PENGUIN CLASSICS

P9-CJL-979

PENGUIN SELECTED ENGLISH POETS
GENERAL EDITOR: CHRISTOPHER RICKS

ROBERT LOUIS STEVENSON:
SELECTED POEMS

ROBERT LOUIS STEVENSON was born in Edinburgh in 1850. The son of a prosperous civil engineer, he was expected to follow the family profession but finally was allowed to study law at Edinburgh University. Stevenson reacted violently against the Presbyterian respectability of the city's professional classes and this led to painful clashes with his parents. In his early twenties he became afflicted with a severe respiratory illness from which he was to suffer for the rest of his life; it was at this time that he determined to become a professional writer. In 1879 he nearly killed himself travelling to California to marry Fanny Osbourne, an American ten years his senior. Together they continued his search for a climate kind to his fragile health, eventually settling in Samoa, where he died on 3 December 1894.

Though the poetry that he wrote all his life often expresses gentle feelings – friendship, nostalgia and humour – Stevenson's Calvinistic upbringing gave him a preoccupation with predestination and a fascination with the presence of evil. In *Dr Jekyll and Mr Hyde* he explores the darker side of the human psyche, and the character of the Master in *The Master of Ballantrae* (1889) was intended to be 'all I know of the Devil'. Stevenson began his literary career as an essayist and travel-writer, but the success of *Treasure Island* (1883) and *Kidnapped* (1886) established his reputation for tales of action and adventure. *Kidnapped*, and its sequel *Catriona* (1893), *The Master of Ballantrae* and stories such as 'Thrawn Janet' and 'The Merry Men' also reveal his knowledge and feeling for the Scottish cultural past. During the last years of his life Stevenson's creative range developed considerably and *The Beach of Falesá* brought to fiction the kind of scene now associated with Conrad and Maugham. At the time of his death Robert Louis Stevenson was working on *Weir of Hermiston*, at once a romantic historical novel and a reworking of one of Stevenson's own most distressing experiences, the conflict between father and son.

ROBERT LOUIS STEVENSON

Selected Poems

Edited by ANGUS CALDER

PENGUIN BOOKS

PENGUIN BOOKS

Published by the Penguin Group
Penguin Books Ltd, 27 Wrights Lane, London W8 5TZ, England
Penguin Putnam Inc., 375 Hudson Street, New York, New York 10014, USA
Penguin Books Australia Ltd, Ringwood, Victoria, Australia
Penguin Books Canada Ltd, 10 Alcorn Avenue, Toronto, Ontario, Canada M4V 3B2
Penguin Books India (P) Ltd, 11, Community Centre, Panchsheel Park, New Delhi – 110 017, India
Penguin Books (NZ) Ltd, Private Bag 102902, NSMC, Auckland, New Zealand
Penguin Books (South Africa) (Pty) Ltd, 5 Watkins Street, Denver Ext 4, Johannesburg 2094, South Africa

Penguin Books Ltd, Registered Offices: Harmondsworth, Middlesex, England

First published 1998

021

Selection, Preface and Notes copyright © Angus Calder, 1998
All rights reserved

The moral right of the editor has been asserted

Set in 10/11.5pt Monotype Ehrhardt
Typeset by Rowland Phototypesetting Ltd, Bury St Edmunds, Suffolk
Printed in England by Clays Ltd, St Ives plc

www.greenpenguin.co.uk

MIX
Paper from
responsible sources
FSC
www.fsc.org   FSC™ C018179

Penguin Books is committed to a sustainable
future for our business, our readers and our planet.
This book is made from Forest Stewardship
Council™ certified paper.

CONTENTS

FROM *UNDERWOODS* (1887)

FROM *BALLADS* (1890)

UNCOLLECTED POEMS, 1885–1894

FROM *SONGS OF TRAVEL* (1895)

PREFACE

Until his mid twenties, poetry was the main focus of Stevenson's literary aspirations. He was fascinated by verse technique and continued to experiment throughout his life. Greek and Latin classics, the lyrics of Herrick and Jonson, the octosyllabics of Miltons's *L'Allegro* and Marvell, and the *lieder* of Goethe and Heine gave him usable models. He was strongly affected – like every major writer in the Scottish tradition – by the extraordinary power of native folksong, and he employed the 'Standard Habbie' stanza, associated above all with Robert Burns, in both Scots and English. He produced the most anthologized poems in Scots between the death of Hogg in 1835 and the experiments of Hugh MacDiarmid in the 1920s. Whitman inspired him to accomplished free verse. The 'musical' rather than 'literal' inspiration of numerous haunting poems aligns him with the French *symbolistes* who were his contemporaries. If his salient influence was on A. E. Housman and the Georgians, he also anticipated effects found in Yeats, Pound and Auden.

But considered style was applied to personal themes – love (ideal and erotic), nostalgia and cordial friendship – which he could only refract in his prose. Horace and Martial, addressing their as-it-were friends, were important models for him. Poetry was for Stevenson the medium of his most intimate conversations. *Underwoods* and *Songs of Travel* contain poems addressed to individuals and his letters are scattered with verses. To his correspondents, he usually deprecated his own poetic talent and they, and critical posterity, concurred far too readily in the verdict that he was a master storyteller and essayist whose verses were merely an agreeable annexe to his prose *œuvre*. There has been amazingly little significant comment by critics (and even by biographers) on his poems.

Nevertheless, the manuscripts of unpublished poems that he left in plenitude behind him attracted the avid interest of rich collectors. Hence the guddle that Janet Adam Smith cleared up in her 1950 volume, *Collected Poems*. After Stevenson's widow died in 1914, her daughter auctioned the manuscripts in New York. Rich purchasers allowed the Boston Bibliophile Society to print scores of posthumous poems in three handsome but inexpertly edited volumes, 1916–21, for the delectation of its own members, where drafts and obvious discards jostled with good finished work. As Stevenson's American and British publishers regained control, they shovelled the Bostonian discoveries into collected editions of his works – the limited Vailima of 1922 and the popular Tusitala of 1923 – higgledy-piggledy, without regard for chronology, along with items independently retrieved by various editors at various times. Janet Adam Smith, by valiant and erudite scouting, produced sound texts and arranged them to clarify Stevenson's development as a poet.

Janet Adam Smith's volume, lightly updated in a second edition in 1971, is an underrated masterpiece of scholarship. But it provides her 'collection', not a 'complete' Stevenson. She printed in full the three volumes that Stevenson published in his lifetime and the posthumous *Songs of Travel* planned by Stevenson and seen through the press, it would seem loyally, by his friend Sidney Colvin. She selected rigorously from the rest. She also fissured chronology by putting into a separate section what she considered 'Light Verse', as with Stevenson's 'Poems for Children'. With such a mercurial, witty writer, 'lightness' is hard to distinguish. The *Child's Garden* collection of 1885 was a major achievement, which, like the Tales of Beatrix Potter, has gratified generations of parents, probably much more than their young charges: it is a masterpiece *about* childhood, childhood fears and loneliness, and childhood vision.

In our Time of the Breaking of Canons, the present selection assimilates 'light' verse and places the *Child's Garden*, complete, in chronological position. It includes four poems rejected by Janet Adam Smith, and amends her chronology with the help of Bradford Booth and Ernest Mehew's imposing new eight-volume edition of Stevenson's letters. However, I have followed Janet Adam Smith's text, with a few small emendations, barring the four exceptions, where I have checked early readings against the Tusitala Edition. My annotations aim to clarify dates and, where known, circumstances of the production of the poems. My aim is to reintroduce readers to a poet whom most know from a dozen or score of justly much-anthologized pieces. Stevenson's verse is very varied and provides many kinds of pleasure and interest beside the pre-Yeatsian 'folk' idiom of 'The Spaewife' and the inimitable plangency of 'Requiem'.

ACKNOWLEDGEMENTS

I would particularly like to thank Jenni Calder and Ian Campbell for advice, Isla Calder for help in preparing this edition for press, and Paul Keegan and Christopher Ricks for acute editorial comments.

TABLE OF DATES

December: London and Cambridge with Colvin.

1875 February: Meets the English poet W. E. Henley, a patient in Edinburgh Infirmary.

March–April: Visits artists' colonies in France with Bob.

July: Admitted – an advocate – to the Scottish Bar. On return to France meets Mrs Fanny Van de Grift Osbourne, ten years older than himself, a student of art with an estranged husband in California, a nearly grown daughter Isobel and small son Lloyd.

September: Back in Edinburgh.

1876 January: Walking tour in south-west Scotland.

April–May: London.

August–October: Canoe trip in Belgium and France with Simpson – 'an inland voyage'.

Autumn: France – Grez and Barbizon.

1877 January–February: London.

June onwards: Almost continuously in France until March 1878.

1878 April–May: Edinburgh. *An Inland Voyage* – first book – published in May.

June: Paris, as secretary to Fleeming Jenkin of Edinburgh University, a juror at the Exposition – the only salaried post RLS ever held.

August: London and Paris. Fanny Osbourne returns to America.

September–October: Walking trip in the Cevennes.

October–December: London. *Edinburgh: Picturesque Notes* published (December).

1879 January: Swanston with Henley, writing *Deacon Brodie*.

February and May: London.

June: Cernay-la-Ville in France. *Travels with a Donkey* published.

July: Edinburgh and London.

August: Embarks for America.

September–December: With Fanny Osbourne and her family in Monterey, California.

December: Till May 1880, living in San Francisco (Fanny in Oakland).

1880 19 May: Marries Fanny in San Francisco.

June–July: Honeymoon in Silverado, Napa County.

August: Returns to Britain with Fanny and Lloyd.

August–September: Strathpeffer (a spa in the north of Scotland) and Edinburgh.

November: Till April, in Davos, Switzerland. Meets poet and man of letters, John Addington Symonds, and his friend H. F. Brown.

1881: April: *Virginibus Puerisque* published.

June–July: Pitlochry (Perthshire).

August–September: Braemar (Aberdeenshire).

October: Again in Davos, till April 1882.

1882 March: *Familiar Studies of Men and Books* published.

April–June: London and Edinburgh.

June–July: Stobo Manse, near Peebles (Scottish Border country).

July–August: Kingussie (Perthshire). *New Arabian Nights* published in August.

September: In France with Bob, looking for a home – joined by Fanny in Marseilles.

October: Campagne Defli, St Marcel, near Marseilles.

December: Marseilles and Nice.

1883 March: Chalet, 'La Solitude', at Hyères, inland from Nice.

July–August: Royat.

December: *The Silverado Squatters* and *Treasure Island* published.

1884 January: RLS, long subject to haemorrhages, very ill in Nice. 'For the next five years, until he reached southern Pacific waters, Louis was liable to sudden illness at any time. Nowhere, neither in France nor the South of England, was he free from the likelihood of haemorrhage, fever and debilitation.' (Jenni Calder, *RLS: A Life Study*, p. 183.)

February: Returns to Hyères.

June–July: Royat.

Late summer: Bournemouth.

1885 Spring: Thomas Stevenson gives a house in Bournemouth, 'Skerryvore', to Fanny. The Stevensons settle there.

March: *A Child's Garden of Verses* published.

May: *More New Arabian Nights*, with Fanny, published.

November: *Prince Otto* published.

1886 January: *Dr Jekyll and Mr Hyde* published.
July: *Kidnapped* published.
November: With Colvin in London.

1887 May: In Edinburgh, for death of Thomas Stevenson. RLS depressed for several months.
August: 'My spirits are rising again ... I almost begin to feel as if I should care to live ...' (*Letters*, V; to Henley). *Underwoods* published. Sails for America with Fanny, Lloyd and widowed mother on 22 August.
September: Newport, RI, then settles at Saranac, NY.
December: *Memories and Portraits* published.

1888 April: New York City.
May: Manasquan, NJ.
June: San Francisco. 28 June, sets out on first Pacific voyage, on the *Casco*.
July–August: Marquesan Islands.
September: Paumotu Islands.
October: Society Islands (Tahiti). Stays with sub-chief Ori.
December: Sandwich Islands, then, till June 1889, Honolulu.

1889 June: *The Wrong Box* (with Lloyd Osbourne) published. Sets out on second cruise, aboard the *Equator*, to the Gilbert Islands.
September: *The Master of Ballantrae* published.
December: In Samoa, purchases estate, Vailima.

1890 February: Sydney.
April–August: Third cruise, on *Janet Nicoll*, to Gilberts, Marshalls, etc.
August–September: Sydney.
October: Settles in Samoa.
December: *Ballads* published.

1891 January: To Sydney, to meet mother returning from Scotland.

1892 April: *Across the Plains* published.
August: *A Footnote to History* published.

1893 February: Sydney.
April: *Island Nights' Entertainments* published.
August: Outbreak of war on Samoa.
September–October: Honolulu. *Catriona* published.
November: Returns to Vailima.

FURTHER READING

EDITIONS

Janet Adam Smith, ed., *Robert Louis Stevenson – Collected Poems* (London, 1950; revised edition 1971).
Robert Louis Stevenson, *The Works of Robert Louis Stevenson*, Tusitala Edition, *Poems*, Vols. I and II (London, [1923]).

LETTERS

Bradford A. Booth and Ernest Mehew, eds., *Letters of Robert Louis Stevenson*, 8 vols. (New Haven, 1994–6).

BIOGRAPHY

Graham Balfour, *The Life of Robert Louis Stevenson*, 2 vols. (London, 1901).
J. C. Furnas, *Voyage to Windward* (London, 1952).
David Daiches, *Robert Louis Stevenson and His World* (London, 1973).
Jenni Calder, *RLS: A Life Study* (London, 1980).
Ian Bell, *Dreams of Exile: Robert Louis Stevenson* (Edinburgh, 1992).
Frank McLynn, *Robert Louis Stevenson: A Biography* (London, 1993).

CRITICISM AND SCHOLARSHIP

There has been a vast amount of critical discussion of Stevenson's fiction, and very little indeed of his verse. Early judgements can be found in:

Paul Maixner, ed., *Robert Louis Stevenson: The Critical Heritage* (London, 1971).

Since these, the most notable contribution, along with Janet Adam Smith's lengthy Introduction to her *Collected Poems*, is:

Edwin Morgan, 'The Poetry of Robert Louis Stevenson' in *Essays* (Manchester, 1974).

UNCOLLECTED POEMS, TO 1885

The Light-Keeper

I

The brilliant kernel of the night,
The flaming lightroom circles me:
I sit within a blaze of light
Held high above the dusky sea.
Far off the surf doth break and roar
Along bleak miles of moonlit shore,
Where through the tides the tumbling wave
Falls in an avalanche of foam
And drives its churned waters home
Up many an undercliff and cave.

The clear bell chimes: the clockworks strain,
The turning lenses flash and pass,
Frame turning within glittering frame
With frosty gleam of moving glass:
Unseen by me, each dusky hour
The sea-waves welter up the tower
Or in the ebb subside again;
And ever and anon all night,
Drawn from afar by charm of light,
A sea bird beats against the pan.

And lastly when dawn ends the night
And belts the semi-orb of sea,
The tall, pale pharos in the light
Looks white and spectral as may be.
The early ebb is out: the green
Straight belt of seaweed now is seen,
That round the basement of the tower
Marks out the interspace of tide;
And watching men are heavy-eyed,
And sleepless lips are dry and sour.

The night is over like a dream:
The sea-birds cry and dip themselves:
And in the early sunlight, steam
The newly bared and dripping shelves,
Around whose verge the glassy wave
With lisping wash is heard to lave;
While, on the white tower lifted high,
The circling lenses flash and pass
With yellow light in faded glass
40   And sickly shine against the sky.

II

As the steady lenses circle
With a frosty gleam of glass;
And the clear bell chimes,
And the oil brims over the lip of the burner,
Quiet and still at his desk,
The lonely Light-Keeper
Holds his vigil.

Lured from far,
The bewildered seagull beats
50   Dully against the lantern;
Yet he stirs not, lifts not his head
From the desk where he reads,
Lifts not his eyes to see
The chill blind circle of night
Watching him through the panes.
This is his country's guardian,
The outmost sentry of peace.
This is the man
Who gives up that is lovely in living
60   For the means to live.

Poetry cunningly gilds
The life of the Light-Keeper,
Held on high in the blackness
In the burning kernel of night,
The seaman sees and blesses him,

The Poet, deep in a sonnet,
Numbers his inky fingers
Fitly to praise him.
Only we behold him,
70   Sitting, patient and stolid,
Martyr to a salary.

'The roadside lined with ragweed, the sharp hills'

The roadside lined with ragweed, the sharp hills
     Standing against the glow of eve, the patch
Of rough white oats 'mongst darkling granite knolls,
     The ferny coverts where the adders hatch,
The hollow that the northern sea upfills,
     The seagull wheeling by with strange, sad calls,
All these, this evening, weary me. Full fain
     Would I turn up the little elm tree way
And under the last elm tree, once again
10   Stretch myself with my head among the grass;
     So lying, tyne the memories of day
     And let my loosed, insatiate being pass
Into the blackbird's song of summer ease,
Or, with the white moon, rise in spirit from the trees.

Spring-Song

The air was full of sun and birds,
     The fresh air sparkled clearly.
Remembrance wakened in my heart
     And I knew I loved her dearly.

The fallows and the leafless trees
     And all my spirit tingled.
My earliest thought of love, and spring's
     First puff of perfume mingled.

In my still heart, the thoughts awoke
10   Came bone by bone together –
Say, birds and sun and spring, is love
        A mere affair of weather?

Duddingston

I

With caws and chirrupings, the woods
    In this thin sun rejoice,
The Psalm seems but the little kirk
    That sings with its own voice.

The cloud-rifts share their amber light
    With the surface of the mere –
I think the very stones are glad
    To feel each other near.

Once more my whole heart leaps and swells
10   And gushes o'er with glee:
The fingers of the sun and shade
    Touch music stops in me.

II

Now fancy paints that bygone day
    When you were here, my fair –
The whole lake rang with rapid skates
    In the windless, winter air.

You leaned to me, I leaned to you,
    Our course was smooth as flight –
We steered – a heel-touch to the left,
20   A heel-touch to the right.

We swung our way through flying men,
    Your hand lay fast in mine,
We saw the shifting crowd dispart,
    The level ice-reach shine.

I swear by yon swan-travelled lake,
    By yon calm hill above,
I swear had we been drowned that day
    We had been drowned in love.

'The whole day thro', in contempt and pity'

The whole day thro', in contempt and pity,
    I pass your houses and beat my drum,
    In the roar of people that go and come,
In the sunlit streets of the city.

Hark! do you hear the ictus coming,
    Mid the roar and clatter of feet?
    Hark! in the ebb and flow of the street
Do you hear the sound of my drumming?

Sun and the fluttering ribbons blind me;
    But still I beat as I travel the town,
    And still the recruits come manfully down,
And the march grows long behind me.

In time to the drum the feet fall steady,
    The feet fall steady and firm to hear,
    And we cry, as we march, that the goal is near,
For all men are heroes already!

'I sit up here at midnight'

I sit up here at midnight,
  The wind is in the street,
The rain besieges the windows
  Like the sound of many feet.

I see the street lamps flicker,
  I see them wink and fail,
The streets are wet and empty,
  It blows an easterly gale.

Some think of the fisher skipper
  Beyond the Inchcape stone;
But I of the fisher woman
  That lies at home alone.

She raises herself on her elbow
  And watches the firelit floor;
Her eyes are bright with terror,
  Her heart beats fast and sore.

Between the roar of the flurries,
  When the tempest holds his breath
She holds her breathing also —
  It is all as still as death.

She can hear the cinders dropping,
  The cat that purrs in its sleep —
The foolish fisher woman!
  Her heart is on the deep.

Dedication

My first gift and my last, to you
I dedicate this fascicle of songs –
The only wealth I have:
Just as they are, to you.

I speak the truth in soberness, and say
I had rather bring a light to your clear eyes,
Had rather hear you praise
This bosomful of trifles,

Than that the whole, hard world with one consent,
In one continuous chorus of applause
Poured forth for me and mine
The homage of due praise.

I write the *finis* here against my love,
This is my love's last epitaph and tomb.
Here the road forks, and I
Go my way, far from yours.

Epistle to Charles Baxter

Repeated grain should fill the reaper's grange,
My fate for thine I would not change.
Thy pathway would to me be strange,
    And strange to thee
The limits of the daily range
        That pleases me.

For me, I do but ask such grace
As Icarus. Bright breathing space –
One glorious moment – face to face,
      The sun and he!
The next, fit grave for all his race,
      The splendid sea.

The father, rich in forty years
Of poor experience culled in tears,
Meanly restrained by sordid fears
      Went limping home
And hung his pinions by the spears,
      No more to roam.

O more to me a thousand fold
The son's brief triumph, wisely bold
To separate from the common fold,
      The general curse,
The accustomed way of growing old
      And growing worse.

O happy lot! A heart of fire,
In the full flush of young desire,
Not custom-taught to shun the mire
      And hold the wall,
His sole experience to aspire,
      To soar and fall.

His golden hap it was to go
Straight from the best of life below
To life above. Not his to know,
      O greatly blest,
How deadly weary life can grow
      To e'en the best.

Sad life, whose highest lore, in vain
The nobler summits to attain,
Still bids me draw the kindly strain
        Of love more tight,
And ease my individual pain
        In your delight.

For I, that would be blythe and merry,
Prefer to call Marsala sherry,
When duty-bound to cross the ferry
        Believe it smooth,
And under pleasant fictions bury
        Distasteful truth.

And hence I banish wisdom, set
The sole imperial coronet
On cheerful Folly, at regret
        Pull many a mouth,
Drown care in jovial bouts – and yet
        Sigh for the South!

O South, South, South! O happy land!
Thou beckon'st me with phantom hand.
Sweet Memories at my bedside stand
        All night in tears.
The roar upon thy nightly strand
        Yet fills mine ears.

The young grass sparkles in the breeze,
The pleasant sunshine warms my knees,
The buds are thick upon the trees,
        The clouds float high.
We sit out here in perfect ease –
        My pipe and I.

Fain would I be, where (winter done)
By dusty roads and noontide sun,
The soldiers, straggling one by one,
70   Marched disarrayed
And spoiled the hedge, till every gun
          A Rose displayed.

Or, O flower-land, I would be where
(The trivial, well-beloved affair!)
The bird-watch drew with gentle care
          From up his sleeve
And gave me, fluttering from the snare,
          A *Mange-Olive*.

Aye, dear to me the slightest tie
80 That binds my heart to thee, O high
And sovereign land for whom I sigh
          In pain to see
The Springtime come again, and I
          So far from thee!

But hush! the clear-throat blackbird sings
From haugh and hill the Season brings
Great armfuls of delightful things
          To stop my mouth
Though still (caged-bird) I beat my wings
90   Toward the South.

To Charles Baxter

Blame me not that this epistle
    Is the first you have from me.
          Idleness has held me fettered,
          But at last the times are bettered
And once more I wet my whistle
    Here in France, beside the sea.

All the green and idle weather
  I have had in sun and shower
    Such an easy warm subsistence,
    Such an indolent existence
I should find it hard to sever
  Day from day and hour from hour.

Many a tract-provided ranter
  May upbraid me, dark and sour,
    Many a bland Utilitarian
    Or excited Millenarian,
– 'Pereunt et imputantur
  You must speak to every hour.'

But the very term's deceptive,
  You, at least, my friend, will see,
    That in sunny grassy meadows
    Trailed across by moving shadows
To be actively receptive
  Is as much as man can be.

He that all the winter grapples
  Difficulties, thrust and ward –
    Needs to cheer him thro' his duty
    Memories of sun and beauty,
Orchards with the russet apples
  Lying scattered on the sward.

Many such I keep in prison,
  Keep them here at heart unseen,
    Till my muse again rehearses
    Long years hence, and in my verses
You shall meet them re-arisen
  Ever comely, ever green.

You know how they never perish,
　　How, in time of later art,
　　　　Memories consecrate and sweeten
40　　　　These defaced and tempest-beaten
Flowers of former years we cherish,
　　Half a life, against our heart.

Most, those love-fruits withered greenly,
　　Those frail, sickly amourettes,
　　　　How they brighten with the distance
　　　　Take new strength and new existence
Till we see them sitting queenly
　　Crowned and courted by regrets!

All that loveliest and best is,
50　　Aureole-fashion round their heads,
　　　　They that looked in life but plainly,
　　　　How they stir our spirits vainly
When they come to us Alcestis-
　　Like, returning from the dead!

Not the old love but another,
　　Bright she comes at Memory's call
　　　　Our forgotten vows reviving
　　　　To a newer, livelier living,
As the dead child to the mother
60　　Seems the fairest child of all.

Thus our Goethe, sacred master,
　　Travelling backward thro' his youth,
　　　　Surely wandered wrong in trying
　　　　To renew the old, undying
Loves that cling in memory faster
　　Than they ever lived in truth.

To Sydney

Not thine where marble-still and white
Old statues share the tempered light
And mock the uneven modern flight,
      But in the stream
Of daily sorrow and delight
      To seek a theme.

I too, O friend, have steeled my heart
Boldly to choose the better part,
To leave the beaten ways of art
10   And wholly free
To dare, beyond the scanty chart,
      The deeper sea.

All vain restrictions left behind,
Frail bark! I loose my anchored mind
And large, before the prosperous wind
      Desert the strand –
A new Columbus sworn to find
      The morning land.

Nor too ambitious, friend. To thee
20 I own my weakness. Not for me
To sing the enfranchised nations' glee,
      Or count the cost
Of warships foundered far at sea
      And battles lost.

High on the far-seen, sunny hills,
Morning-content my bosom fills;
Well-pleased, I trace the wandering rills
      And learn their birth.
Far off, the clash of sovereign wills
30   May shake the earth.

The nimble circuit of the wheel,
The uncertain poise of merchant weal,
Horror of famine, fire and steel
         When nations fall;
These, heedful, from afar I feel –
         I mark them all.

But not, my friend, not these I sing,
My voice shall fill a narrower ring.
Tired souls, that flag upon the wing,
40   I seek to cheer:
Brave wines to strengthen hope I bring,
         Life's cantineer!

Some song that shall be suppling oil
To weary muscles strained with toil,
Shall hearten for the daily moil,
         Or widely read
Make sweet for him that tills the soil
         His daily bread –

Push gaily on, strong heart! The while
50 You travel forward mile by mile,
He loiters with a backward smile
         Till you can overtake,
And strains his eyes to search his wake,
Or whistling, as he sees you through the brake,
         Waits on a stile.

'O dull, cold northern sky'

O dull, cold northern sky,
   O brawling sabbath bells,
   O feebly twittering Autumn bird that tells
The year is like to die!

O still, spoiled trees, O city ways,
    O sun desired in vain,
    O dread presentiment of coming rain
That clogs the sullen days!

Thee, heart of mine, I greet.
    In what hard mountain pass
    Striv'st thou? In what importunate morass
Sink now thy weary feet?

Thou run'st a hopeless race
    To win despair. No crown
    Awaits success; but leaden gods look down
On thee, with evil face.

And those that would befriend
    And cherish thy defeat,
    With angry welcome shall turn sour the sweet
Home-coming of the end.

Yea, those that offer praise
    To idleness, shall yet
    Insult thee, coming glorious in the sweat
Of honourable ways.

Ne Sit Ancillae Tibi Amor Pudori

There's just a twinkle in your eye
That seems to say I *might*, if I
Were only bold enough to try
    An arm about your waist.

I hear, too, as you come and go,
That pretty nervous laugh, you know;
And then your cap is always so
    Coquettishly displaced.

Your cap! the word's profanely said,
10   That little topknot, white and red,
That quaintly crowns your graceful head,
    No bigger than a flower,

You set with such a witching art,
And so provocatively smart,
I'd like to wear it on my heart,
    An order for an hour!

O graceful housemaid, tall and fair,
I love your shy imperial air,
And always loiter on the stair,
20   When you are going by.

A strict reserve the fates demand;
But, when to let you pass I stand,
Sometimes by chance I touch your hand
    And sometimes catch your eye.

To Ottilie

You remember, I suppose,
How the August sun arose,
    And how his face
Woke to trill and carolette
All the cages that were set
    About the place.

In the tender morning light
All around lay strange and bright
    And still and sweet,
22   And the grey doves unafraid
Went their morning promenade
    Along the street.

'A little before me, and hark!'

A little before me, and hark!
The dogs in the village bark.
And see, in the blank of the dark,
    The eye of a window shine!

There stands the inn, the small and rude,
In this earth's vast robber-wood
The inn with the beds and the food,
    The inn of the shining wine.

We do but bait on life's bare plain,
And through the new day's joy and pain
Reach to the baiting place again.
    O rest, for the night, be mine!

Rest for the night! For to love and rest,
To clasp the hands, to keep the nest,
Are only human at the best:
    To move and to suffer divine.

St Martin's Summer

As swallows turning backward
    When half-way o'er the sea,
At one word's trumpet summons
    They came again to me –
The hopes I had forgotten
    Came back again to me.

I know not which to credit,
    O lady of my heart!
Your eyes that bade me linger,
    Your words that bade us part –
I know not which to credit,
    My reason or my heart.

But be my hopes rewarded,
  Or be they but in vain,
I have dreamed a golden vision,
  I have gathered in the grain –
I have dreamed a golden vision,
  I have not lived in vain.

'My brain swims empty and light'

My brain swims empty and light
Like a nut on a sea of oil;
And an atmosphere of quiet
Wraps me about from the turmoil and clamour of life.

I stand apart from living,
Apart and holy I stand,
In my new-gained growth of idleness, I stand,
As stood the Shekinah of yore in the holy of holies.

I walk the streets smoking my pipe
And I love the dallying shop-girl
That leans with rounded stern to look at the fashions;
And I hate the bustling citizen,
The eager and hurrying man of affairs I hate,
Because he bears his intolerance writ on his face
And every movement and word of him tells me how much
    he hates me.

I love night in the city,
The lighted streets and the swinging gait of harlots.
I love cool pale morning,
In the empty bye-streets,
With only here and there a female figure,
A slavey with lifted dress and the key in her hand,
A girl or two at play in a corner of waste-land
Tumbling and showing their legs and crying out to me loosely.

The Cruel Mistress

Here let me rest, here nurse the uneasy qualm
That yearns within me;
And to the heaped-up sea,
Sun-spangled in the quiet afternoon,
Sing my devotions.

In the sun, at the edge of the down,
The whin-pods crackle
In desultory volleys;
And the bank breathes in my face
10   Its hot sweet breath –
Breath that stirs and kindles,
Lights that suggest, not satisfy –
Is there never in life or nature
An opiate for desire?
Has everything here a voice,
Saying '*I am not the goal;*
Nature is not to be looked at alone;
Her breath, like the breath of a mistress,
Her breath also,
20   *Parches the spirit with longing*
Sick and enervating longing.'

Well, let the matter rest.
I rise and brush the windle-straws
Off my clothes; and lighting another pipe
Stretch myself over the down.
Get thee behind me, Nature!
I turn my back on the sun
And face from the grey new town at the foot of the bay.

I know an amber lady
30   Who has her abode
     At the lips of the street
In prisons of coloured glass.
I had rather die of her love

Than sicken for you, O Nature!
Better be drunk and merry
Than dreaming awake!
Better be Falstaff than Obermann!

Storm

The narrow lanes are vacant and wet;
The rough wind bullies and blusters about the township.
And spins the vane on the tower
And chases the scurrying leaves,
And the straw in the damp innyard.
See – a girl passes
Tripping gingerly over the pools,
And under her lifted dress
I catch the gleam of a comely, stockinged leg.
10   Pah! the room stifles me,
Reeking of stale tobacco –
With the four black mealy horrible prints
After Landseer's pictures.
I will go out.

Here the free wind comes with a fuller circle,
Sings, like an angry wasp, in the straining grass,
Sings and whistles;
And the hurried flow of rain
Scourges my face and passes.
20   Behind me, clustered together, the rain-wet roofs of the town
Shine, and the light vane shines as it veers
In the long pale finger of sun that hurries across them to me.
The fresh salt air is keen in my nostrils,
And far down the shining sand
Foam and thunder
And take the shape of the bay in eager mirth
The white-head hungry billows.
The earth shakes
As the semicircle of waters

30 Stoops and casts itself down;
And far outside in the open,
Wandering gleams of sunshine
Show us the ordered horde that hurries to follow.

Ei! merry companions,
Your madness infects me.
My whole soul rises and falls and leaps and tumbles with you!
I shout aloud and incite you, O white-headed merry
        companions.
The sight of you alone is better than drinking.
The brazen band is loosened from off my forehead;
40 My breast and my brain are moistened and cool;
And still I yell in answer
To your hoarse inarticulate voices,
O big, strong, bullying, boisterous waves,
That are of all things in nature the nearest thoughts to human,
Because you are wicked and foolish,
Mad and destructive.

Stormy Nights

I cry out war to those who spend their utmost,
Trying to substitute a vain regret
For childhood's vanished moods,
Instead of a full manly satisfaction
In new development.
Their words are vain as the lost shouts,
The wasted breath of solitary hunters
That are far buried in primeval woods –
Clamour that dies in silence,
10 Cries that bring back no answer
But the great voice of the wind-shaken forest,
Mocking despair.

No – they will get no answer;
For I too recollect,
I recollect and love my perished childhood,
Perfectly love and keenly recollect;
I too remember; and if it could be
Would not recall it.

Do I not know, how, nightly, on my bed
20   The palpable close darkness shutting round me,
How my small heart went forth to evil things,
How all the possibilities of sin
That were yet present to my innocence
Bound me too narrowly,
And how my spirit beat
The cage of its compulsive purity;
How – my eyes fixed,
My shot lip tremulous between my fingers
I fashioned for myself new modes of crime,
30   Created for myself with pain and labour
The evil that the cobwebs of society,
The comely secrecies of education,
Had made an itching mystery to meward.

Do I not know again,
When the great winds broke loose and went abroad
At night in the lighted town –
Ah! then it was different –
Then, when I seemed to hear
The storm go by me like a cloak-wrapt horseman
40   Stooping over the saddle –
Go by, and come again and yet again,
Like some one riding with a pardon,
And ever baffled, ever shut from passage:
Then when the house shook and a horde of noises
Came out and clattered over me all night,
Then, would my heart stand still,
My hair creep fearfully upon my head
And, with my tear-wet face
Buried among the bed-clothes,
50   Long and bitterly would I pray and wrestle

Till gentle sleep
Threw her great mantle over me,
And my heard breathing gradually ceased.

I was then the Indian,
Well and happy and full of glee and pleasure,
Both hands full of life.
And not without divine impulses
Shot into me by the untried non-ego;
But, like the Indian, too,
60   Not yet exempt from feverish questionings,
And on my bed of leaves,
Writhing terribly in grasp of terror,
As when the still stars and the great white moon
Watch me athwart black foliage,
Trembling before the interminable vista,
The widening wells of space
In which my thought flags like a wearied bird
In the mid ocean of his autumn flight –
Prostrate before the indefinite great spirit
70   That the external warder
Plunged like a dagger
Into my bosom.
Now, I am a Greek
White-robed among the sunshine and the statues
And the fair porticos of carven marble –
Fond of olives and dry sherry,
Good tobacco and clever talk with my fellows,
Free from inordinate cravings.
Why would you hurry me, O evangelist,
80   You with the bands and the shilling packet of tracts
Greatly reduced when taken for distribution?
Why do you taunt my progress,
O green-spectacled Wordsworth! in beautiful verses,
You, the elderly poet?
So I shall travel forward
Step by step with the rest of my race,
In time, if death should spare me,
I shall come on to a farther stage,
And show you St Francis of Assisi.

Song at Dawn

I see the dawn creep round the world,
Here damm'd a moment backward by great hills,
There racing o'er the sea.
Down at the round equator,
It leaps forth straight and rapid,
Driving with firm sharp edge the night before it.
Here gradually it floods
The wooded valleys and the weeds
And the still smokeless cities.
10   The cocks crow up at the farms;
The sick man's spirit is glad;
The watch treads brisker about the dew-wet deck;
The light-keeper locks his desk,
As the lenses turn,
Faded and yellow.

The girl with the embroidered shift
Rises and leans on the sill,
And her full bosom heaves
Drinking deep of the silentness.
20   I too rise and watch
The healing fingers of dawn —
I too drink from its eyes
The unaccountable peace —
I too drink and am satisfied as with food.
Fain would I go
Down by the winding crossroad by the trees,
Where at the corner of wet wood
The blackbird in the early grey and stillness
Wakes his first song.

30   Peace who can make verses clink,
Find ictus following surely after ictus
At such an hour as this, the heart
Lies steeped and silent.
O dreaming, leaning girl.

Already are the sovereign hill-tops ruddy,
Already the grey passes, the white streak
Brightens above dark woodlands, Day begins.

'I am a hunchback, yellow faced –'

I am a hunchback, yellow faced –
    A hateful sight to see –
Tis all that other men can do
    To pass and let me be.

I am a woman – my hair is white –
    I was a drunkard's lass;
The gin dances in my head –
    I stumble as I pass.

I am a man that God made at first,
    And teachers tried to harm;
Here, hunchback, take my friendly hand –
    Good woman, take my arm.

10

'Last night we had a thunderstorm in style'

Last night we had a thunderstorm in style.
The wild lightning streaked the airs,
As though my God fell down a pair of stairs.
The thunder boomed and bounded all the while;
All cried and sat by water-side and stile –
To mop our brow had been our chief of cares.
I lay in bed with a Voltairean smile,
The terror of good, simple guilty pairs,
And made this rondeau in ironic style,

10   Last night we had a thunderstorm in style.
      Our God the Father fell down-stairs,
      The stark blue lightning went its flight, the while,
      The very rain you might have heard a mile –
      The strenuous faithful buckled to their prayers.

To Charles Baxter [in Lallan]

Noo lyart leaves blaw ower the green,
Reid are the bonny woods o' Dean,
An' here we're back in Embro, frien',
      To pass the winter.
Whilk noo, wi' frosts afore, draws in,
      An' snaws ahint her.

I've seen 's hae days to fricht us a',
The Pentlands poothered weel wi' snaw,
The ways half smoored wi' liquid thaw
10   An' half congealin',
The snell an' scowtherin' northern blaw
      Frae blae Brunteelan'.

I've seen 's been unco sweir to sally
And at the door-cheeks daff an' dally –
Seen 's daidle thus an' shilly-shally
      For near a minute –
Sae cauld the wind blew up the valley,
      The deil was in it! –

Syne spread the silk an' tak the gate,
20   In blast an' blaudin' rain, deil hae 't!
The hale toon glintin', stane an' slate,
      Wi' cauld an' weet,
An' to the Court, gin we 'se be late,
      Bicker oor feet.

And at the Court, tae, aft I saw
Whaur Advocates by twa an' twa
Gang gesterin' end to end the ha'
    In weeg an' goon,
To crack o' what ye wull but Law
30   The hale forenoon.

That muckle ha', maist like a kirk,
I've kent at braid mid-day sae mirk
Ye'd seen white weegs an' faces lurk
    Like ghaists frae Hell,
But whether Christian ghaists or Turk
    Deil ane could tell.

The three fires lunted in the gloom,
The wind blew like the blast o' doom,
The rain upo' the roof abune
40   Played Peter Dick –
Ye wad nae'd licht enough i' the room
    Your teeth to pick!

But, freend, ye ken how me an' you,
The ling-lang lanely winter through,
Keep'd a guid speerit up, an' true
    To lore Horatian,
We aye the ither bottle drew –
    To inclination.

Sae let us in the comin' days
50 Stand sicker on oor auncient ways –
The strauchtest road in a' the maze
    Since Eve ate apples;
An' let the winter weet oor cla'es –
    We'll weet oor thrapples.

To the Same

On the death of their common friend, Mr John Adam, Clerk of Court

An' Johnie's deid. The mair's the pity!
He's deid, an' deid o' Aqua-vitae.
O Embro', you're a shrunken city,
    Noo Johnie's deid!
Tak hands, an' sing a burial ditty
    Ower Johnie's heid.

To see him was baith drink an' meat,
Gaun linkin' glegly up the street.
He but to rin or tak a seat,
10   The wee bit body!
Bein' aye unsicker on his feet
    Wi' whusky toddy.

To be aye tosh was Johnie's whim.
There's nane was better tent than him,
Though whiles his gravit-knot wad clim'
    Ahint his ear,
An' whiles he'd buttons oot or in
    The less or mair.

His hair a' lank aboot his bree,
20 His tap-lip lang by inches three –
A slockened sort o' mou', to pree
    A' sensuality –
A drouthy glint was in his e'e
    An' personality.

An' day an' nicht, frae daw to daw,
Dink an' perjink an' doucely braw,
Wi' a kind o' Gospel look ower a',
    May or October,
Like Peden, followin' the Law
30   An' no that sober.

An' wow! but John was unco sport.
Whiles he wad smile aboot the Court
Malvolio-like – whiles snore an' snort,
        Was heard afar.
The idle writer lads' resort
        Was aye John's bar.

Whusky an' he were pack thegether.
Whate'er the hour, whate'er the weather,
John kept himsel' wi' mistened leather
        An' kindled spunk.
40 Wi' him, there was nae askin' whether –
        John was aye drunk.

The auncient heroes gash an' bauld
In the uncanny days of Auld,
The task ance found to which th'were called,
        Stack stenchly to it.
His life sic noble lives recalled,
        Little's he knew it.

Single an' straucht, he went his way.
50 He kept the faith an' played the play.
Whusky an' he were man an' may
        Whate'er betided.
Bonny in life – in death, thir twae
        Were no' divided.

What's merely humourous or bonny
The warl' regairds wi' cauld astony.
Drunk men tak aye mair place than ony;
        An' sae, ye see,
The gate was aye ower thrang for Johnie –
60   Or you an' me.

John micht hae jingled cap an' bells,
Been a braw fule in silks an' fells,
In ane o' the auld warl's canty hells,

Paris or Sodom.
I wadnae had him naething else
        But Johnie Adam.

He suffered – as have a' that wan
Eternal memory frae man,
Sin' e'er the weary warl' began –
        Mister or Madam,
Keats or Scots Burns, the Spanish Dan
        Or Johnie Adam.

70

We leuch, an' Johnie deid. An', fegs!
Hoo he had keept his stoiterin' legs
Sae lang's he did, 's a fact that begs
        An explanation.
He stachers fifty years – syne flegs
        To's destination.

'I saw red evening through the rain'

I saw red evening through the rain,
Lower above the steaming plain;
I heard the hour strike small and still,
From the black belfry on the hill.

Thought is driven out of doors to-night
By bitter memory of delight;
The sharp constraint of finger tips,
Or the shuddering touch of lips.

I heard the hour strike small and still,
From the black belfry on the hill.
Behind me I could still look down
On the outspread monstrous town.

10

The sharp constraint of finger tips
Or the shuddering touch of lips,
And all old memories of delight
Crowd upon my soul to-night.

Behind me I could still look down
On the outspread feverish town;
But before me still and grey
20   And lonely was the forward way.

'I who all the winter through'

I who all the winter through,
   Cherished other loves than you,
And kept hands with hoary policy in marriage bed and pew;
   Now I know the false and true,
   For the earnest sun looks through,
And my old love comes to meet me in the dawning and
      the dew.

Now the hedged meads renew
   Rustic odour, smiling hue,
And the clean air shines and twinkles as the world goes
      wheeling through;
10   And my heart springs up anew,
   Bright and confident and true,
And my old love comes to meet me in the dawning and
      the dew.

John Cavalier

These are your hills, John Cavalier.
Your father's kids you tended here,
And grew, among these mountains wild,
A humble and religious child.

Fate turned the wheel; you grew and grew;
Bold Marshals doffed the hat to you;
God whispered counsels in your ear
To guide your sallies, Cavalier.

You shook the earth with martial tread;
The ensigns fluttered by your head;
In Spain or France, Velay or Kent,
The music sounded as you went.
Much would I give if I might spy
Your brave battalions marching by;
Or, on the wind, if I might hear
Your drums and bugles, Cavalier.

In vain. O'er all the windy hill,
The ways are void, the air is still,
Alone, below the echoing rock,
The shepherd calls upon his flock.
The wars of Spain and of Cevennes,
The bugles and the marching men,
The horse you rode for many a year –
Where are they now, John Cavalier?

All armies march the selfsame way
Far from the cheerful eye of day;
And you and yours marched down below
About two hundred years ago.
Over the hills, into the shade,
Journeys each mortal cavalcade;
Out of the sound, out of the sun,
They go when their day's work is done;
And all shall doff the bandoleer
To sleep with dead John Cavalier.

Alcaics to H. F. Brown

Brave lads in olden musical centuries
Sang, night by night, adorable choruses,
   Sat late by ale-house doors in April
Chaunting in joy as the moon was rising.

Moon-seen and merry, under the trellises,
Flush-faced they played with old polysyllables
   Spring scents inspired, old wine diluted,
Love and Apollo were there to chorus.

Now these, the songs, remain to eternity,
Those only, those, the bountiful choristers
   Gone – those are gone, those unremembered
Sleep and are silent in earth forever.

So man himself appears and evanishes,
So smiles and goes; as wanderers halting at
   Some green-embowered house, play their music,
Play and are gone on the windy highway;

Yet dwells the strain enshrined in the memory
Long after they departed eternally,
   Forth-faring toward far mountain summits
Cities of men or the sounding Ocean.

Youth sang the song in years immemorial
Brave chanticleer he sang and was beautiful;
   Bird-haunted, green tree-tops in April
Heard and were pleased by the voice of singing.

Youth goes and leaves behind him a prodigy –
Songs sent by thee afar from Venetian
   Sea-grey lagunes, sea-paven highways,
Dear to me here in my Alpine exile.

Lines for H. F. Brown

Yes, I remember, and still remember wailing
Wind in the clouds and rainy sea-horizon,
Empty and lit with low, nocturnal glimmer,
How in the strong, deep-plunging, transatlantic
Emigrant ship we sang our songs in chorus.
Piping, the gull flew by, the roaring billows
Yawned and resounded round the mighty vessel
Infinite uproar, endless contradiction;
Yet over all our chorus rose reminding
10   Wanderers here at sea of unforgotten
Homes and undying, old, memorial loves.

Brown in his haste demanded this from me.
I in my leisure made the present verse.

To Mrs MacMorland

Im Schnee der Alpen – so it runs
    To those divine accords – and here
We dwell in Alpine snows and suns
    A motley crew, for half the year:
A motley crew we dwell, to taste –
    A shivering band in hope and fear –
That sun upon the snowy waste,
    That Alpine ether cold and clear.

Up from the laboured plain, and up
10   From low sea-levels, we arise
To drink of that diviner cup,
    The rarer air, the clearer skies;
Far, as the great, old, godly King
    From mankind's turbid valley cries,
So all we mountain-lovers sing:
    I to the hills will lift mine eyes!

The bells that ring, the peaks that climb,
   The frozen snow's unbroken curd,
Might well revindicate in rhyme
20   The pauseless stream, the absent bird:
In vain – for to the deeps of life
   You, lady, you, my heart have stirred;
And since you say you love my wife,
   Be sure I love you for the word.

Of kindness, here, I nothing say –
   Such loveless kindnesses there are
In that grimacing, common way,
   That old, unhonoured social war:
Love but my dog and love my love
30   Adore with me a common star –
I value not the rest above
   The ashes of a bad cigar.

Brasheanna

Sonnets on Peter Brash, a publican, dedicated to Charles Baxter

I

We found him first as in the dells of May
   The dreaming damsel finds the earliest flower;
   Thoughtless we wandered in the evening hour;
Aimless and pleased we went our random way:
In the foot-haunted city in the night,
   Among the alternate lamps, we went and came
   Till, like a humourous thunderbolt, that name,
The hated name of BRASH, assailed our sight.
We saw, we paused, we entered, seeking gin.
10   His wrath, like a huge breaker on the beach,
     Broke instant forth. He on the counter beat
     In his infantile fury; and his feet
Danced impotent wrath upon the floor within.
   Still as we fled, we heard his idiot screech

II

We found him and we lost. The glorious BRASH
    Fell as the cedar on the mountain side
    When the resounding thunders far and wide
Redoubling grumble, and the instant flash
Divides the night a moment and is gone;
    He fell not unremembered nor unwept;
    And the dim shop where that great hero slept
Is sacred still. We, steering past the *Tron*
And past the *College* southward, and thy square
    Fitz-Symon! reach at last that holier clime,
And do with tears behold that pot-house, where
        BRASH the divine once ministered in drink,
        Where BRASH, the *Beershop Hornet*, bowed by time,
        In futile anger grinned across the zinc.

III

There let us often wend our pensive way,
    There often pausing celebrate the past;
    For though indeed our BRASH be dead at last,
Perchance his spirit, in some minor way,
Nor pure immortal nor entirely dead,
    Contrives upon the farther shore of death
    To pick a rank subsistence, and for breath
Breathes ague, and drinks creosote of lead,
There, on the way to that infernal den,
    Where burst the flames forth thickly, and the sky
        Flares horrid through the murk methinks he doles
        Damned liquors out to Hellward-faring souls,
    And as his impotent anger ranges high
Gibbers and gurgles at the shades of men.

IV

Alas! that while the beautiful and strong,
    The pious and the wise, the grave and gay,
    All journey downward by one common way,
Bewailed and honoured yet with flowers and song,

There must come crowding with that serious throng,
   Jostling the ranks of that discreet array,
   Infirm and scullion spirits of decay,
50 The dull, the droll, the random and the wrong.
An ape in church, an artificial limb
   Tacked to a marble god serene and blind –
   For such as BRASH, high death was not designed,
That canonising rite was not for him;
   Nor where the Martyr and the Hero trod
   Should idiot BRASH go hobbling up to God.

v

To Goodness or Greatness: to be good and die,
   Or to be great and live forever great:
   To be the unknown Smith that saves the state
60 And blooms unhonoured by the public eye:
To be the unknown Robinson or Brown
   Whose piping virtues perish in the mud
   Or triumphing in blasphemy and blood,
The imperial pirate, pickled in renown:
Unfaltering BRASH the latter number chose
   Of this eterne antithesis: and still
The flower of his immortal memory blows
Where'er the spirits of the loathed repose
   Where'er the trophy of the gibbet hill
70 Dejects the traveller and collects the crows.

'Since years ago for evermore'

Since years ago for evermore
My cedar ship I drew to shore;
And to the road and river-bed
And the green, nodding reeds, I said
Mine ignorant and last farewell:
Now with content at home I dwell,
And now divide my sluggish life
Betwixt my verses and my wife:

In vain: for when the lamp is lit
10   And by the laughing fire I sit,
Still with the tattered atlas spread
Interminable roads I tread.

RHYMES TO W. E. HENLEY

'*Dear Henley, with a pig's snout on*'

Dear Henley, with a pig's snout on
I am starting for London,
Where I likely shall arrive
On Saturday, if still alive:
Perhaps your pirate doctor might
See me on Sunday? If all's right,
I should then lunch with you and with she
Who's dearer to you than you are to me.
I shall remain but little time
10   In London, as a wretched clime,
But not so wretched (for none are)
As that of beastly old Dracmar.
My doctor sends me skipping. I
Have many facts to meet your eye.
My pig's snout now upon my face:
And I inhale with fishy grace,
My gills outflapping right and left,
Ol. pin. sylvest. I am bereft
Of a great deal of charm by this –
20   Not quite the bull's eye for a kiss –
But like the gnome of olden time
Or bogey in a pantomime.
For ladies' love I once was fit,
But now am rather out of it.
Where'er I go, revolted curs
Snap round my military spurs;

The children all retire in fits
And scream their bellowses to bits.
Little I care: the worst's been done:
30   Now let the cold impoverished sun
Drop frozen from his orbit; let
Fury and fire, cold, wind, and wet,
And cataclysmal mad reverses
Rage through the federate universes;
Let Lawson triumph, cakes and ale,
Whiskey and hock and claret fail;
Tobacco, love, and letters perish,
With all that any man could cherish:
You it may touch, not me. I dwell
40   Too deep already – deep in hell;
And nothing can befall, O damn!
To make me uglier than I am.

'My letters fail, I learn with grief, to please'

My letters fail, I learn with grief, to please
Proud spirits that sit and read them at their ease
Not recking how, from an exhausted mind,
By wheel and pulley, tug and strain and grind,
These humble efforts are expressed, like cheese.

'We dwell in these melodious days'

We dwell in these melodious days
When every author trolls his lays;
And all, except myself and you,
Must up and print the nonsense, too.
Why then, if this be so indeed,
If adamantine walls recede
And old Apollo's gardens gape
For Arry and the grinder's ape;

I too may enter in perchance
10   Where paralytic graces dance,
And cheering on each tottering set
Blow my falsetto flageolet.

*   *   *   *   *

Tales of Arabia

Yes, friend, I own these tales of Arabia
Smile not, as smiled their flawless originals
   Age-old but yet untamed, for ages
     Pass and the magic is undiminished.

Thus, friend, the tales of old Camaralzaman,
Ayoub, the Slave of Love, or the Calendars
   Blind-eyed and ill-starred royal scions,
     Charm us in age as they charmed in childhood.

Fair ones, beyond all numerability,
10   Beam from the palace, beam on humanity,
   Bright-eyed, in truth, yet soulless houries
     Offering pleasures and only pleasure.

Thus they, the venal Muses Arabian –
Unlike, indeed, to nobler divinities,
   Greek Gods or old time-honoured muses
     Easily proffer unloved caresses.

Lost, lost, the man who mindeth their minstrelsy;
Since still, in sandy, glittering pleasances,
   Cold, stony fruits, gem-like but quite in-
20   Edible, flatter and wholly starve him.

'Flower god, god of the spring, beautiful, bountiful'

Flower god, god of the spring, beautiful, bountiful,
Gold-dyed shield in the sky, lover of versicles,
    Here I wander in April,
        Cold, grey-headed; and still to my

Heart, Spring comes with a bound, Spring the deliverer,
Spring, song-leader in woods, chorally resonant,
    Spring, flower planter in meadows,
        Child conductor in willowy

Fields deep clotted with bloom, daisies and crocuses:
Here that child from his heart drinks of eternity:
    O child, happy are children!
        She still smiles on their innocence.

She, dear mother in God, fostering violets,
Fills earth full of her scents, voices and violins:
    Thus one cunning in music
        Wakes old chords in the memory:

Thus fair earth in the Spring leads her performances.
One more touch of the bow, smell of the virginal
    Green – one more, and my bosom
        Feels new life with an ecstasy.

'Now bare to the beholder's eye'

Now bare to the beholder's eye,
Your late denuded lendings lie,
Subsiding slowly where they fell,
A disinvested citadel;
The obdurate corset, cupid's foe,
The Dutchman's breeches frilled below.
Hose that the lover loves to note,
And white and crackling petticoat.

From these, that on the ground repose,
10   Their lady lately re-arose;
And laying by the lady's name
A living woman re-became.
Of her, that from the public eye
They do inclose and fortify,
Now, lying scattered as they fell
An indiscreeter tale they tell:
Of that more soft and secret her
Whose daylong fortresses they were,
By fading warmth, by lingering print,
20   These now discarded scabbards hint.

A twofold change the ladies know.
First, in the morn the bugles blow,
And they, with floral hues and scents,
Man their be-ribboned battlements.
But let the stars appear, and they
Shed inhumanities away;
And from the changeling fashion sees,
Through comic and through sweet degrees,
In nature's toilet unsurpassed,
30   Forth leaps the laughing girl at last.

TRANSLATIONS FROM MARTIAL

Epitaphium Erotii

Mother and sire, to you do I commend
Tiny Erotion, who must now descend,
A child, among the shadows, and appear
Before hell's bandog and hell's gondolier.
Of six hoar winters she had felt the cold,
But lacked six days of being six years old.

Now she must come, all playful, to that place
Where the great ancients sit with reverend face;
Now lisping, as she used, of whence she came,
10   Perchance she names and stumbles at my name.
O'er these so fragile bones, let there be laid
A plaything for a turf; and for that maid
That swam light-footed as the thistle-burr
On thee, O Mother earth, be light on her.

De M. Antonio

Now Antonius, in a smiling age,
Counts of his life the fifteenth finished stage.
The rounded days and the safe years he sees
Nor fears death's water mounting round his knees,
To him remembering not one day is sad,
Not one but that its memory makes him glad.
So good men lengthen life; and to recall
The past, is to have twice enjoyed it all.

De Ligurra

You fear, Ligurra – above all, you long –
That I should smite you with a stinging song,
This dreadful honour you both fear and hope:
Both quite in vain: you fall below my scope.
The Libyan lion tears the roaring bull,
He does not harm the midge along the pool.
But if so close this stands in your regard,
From some blind tap fish forth a drunken bard,
Who shall, with charcoal, on the privy wall,
10   Immortalise your name for once and all.

MORAL EMBLEMS (1882)

MORAL EMBLEMS I

I 'See how the children in the print'

See how the children in the print
Bound on the book to see what's in 't!
O, like these pretty babes, may you
Seize and *apply* this volume too!
And while your eye upon the cuts
With harmless ardour opes and shuts,
Reader, may your immortal mind
To their sage lessons not be blind.

II 'Reader, your soul upraise to see'

Reader, your soul upraise to see,
In yon fair cut designed by me,
The pauper by the highwayside
Vainly soliciting from pride.
Mark how the Beau with easy air
Contemns the anxious rustic's prayer,
And casting a disdainful eye,
Goes gaily gallivanting by.
He from the poor averts his head . . .
He will regret it when he's dead.

III A Peak in Darien

Broad-gazing on untrodden lands,
See where adventurous Cortez stands;
While in the heavens above his head,
The Eagle seeks its daily bread.

How aptly fact to fact replies:
Heroes and Eagles, hills and skies.
Ye, who contemn the fatted slave,
Look on this emblem and be brave.

IV 'See in the print, how moved by whim'

See in the print, how moved by whim,
Trumpeting Jumbo, great and grim,
Adjusts his trunk, like a cravat,
To noose that individual's hat.
The sacred Ibis in the distance
Joys to observe his bold resistance.

V 'Mark, printed on the opposing page'

Mark, printed on the opposing page,
The unfortunate effects of rage.
A man (who might be you or me)
Hurls another into the sea.
Poor soul, his unreflecting act
His future joys will much contract;
And he will spoil his evening toddy
By dwelling on that mangled body.

MORAL EMBLEMS II

I 'With storms a-weather, rocks a-lee'

With storms a-weather, rocks a-lee,
The dancing skiff puts forth to sea.
The lone dissenter in the blast
Recoils before the sight aghast.
But she, although the heavens be black,
Holds on upon the starboard tack.
For why? although today she sink
Still safe she sails in printers' ink,
And though today the seamen drown,
My cut shall hand their memory down.

II 'The careful angler chose his nook'

The careful angler chose his nook
At morning by the lilied brook,
And all the noon his rod he plied
By that romantic riverside.
Soon as the evening hours decline
Tranquilly he'll return to dine,
And breathing forth a pious wish,
Will cram his belly full of fish.

III 'The Abbot for a walk went out'

The Abbot for a walk went out
A wealthy cleric, very stout,
And Robin has that Abbot stuck
As the red hunter spears the buck.

The djavel or the javelin
Has, you observe, gone bravely in,
And you may hear that weapon whack
Bang through the middle of his back.
Hence we may learn that abbots should
10   *Never go walking in a wood.*

IV 'The frozen peaks he once explored'

The frozen peaks he once explored,
But now he's dead and by the board.
How better far at home to have stayed
Attended by the parlour maid,
And warmed his knees before the fire
Until the hour when folks retire!
So, if you would be spared to friends,
Do nothing but for business ends.

V 'Industrious pirate! see him sweep'

Industrious pirate! see him sweep
The lonely bosom of the deep,
And daily the horizon scan
From Hatteras or Matapan.
Be sure, before that pirate's old,
He will have made a pot of gold,
And will retire from all his labours
And be respected by his neighbours.
You also scan your life's horizon
10   *For all that you can clap your eyes on.*

FROM *MORAL TALES* [1882]

Robin and Ben: or, the Pirate and the Apothecary

Come lend me an attentive ear
A startling moral tale to hear,
Of Pirate Rob and Chemist Ben,
And different destinies of men.

Deep in the greenest of the vales
That nestle near the coast of Wales,
The heaving main but just in view,
Robin and Ben together grew,
Together worked and played the fool,
Together shunned the Sunday school,
And pulled each other's youthful noses
Around the cots, among the roses.

Together but unlike they grew;
Robin was rough, and through and through,
Bold, inconsiderate, and manly,
Like some historic Bruce or Stanley.
Ben had a mean and servile soul,
He robbed not, though he often stole.
He sang on Sunday in the choir,
And tamely capped the passing Squire.

At length, intolerant of trammels –
Wild as the wild Bithynian camels,
Wild as the wild sea-eagles – Bob
His widowed dam contrives to rob,
And thus with great originality
Effectuates his personality.
Thenceforth his terror-haunted flight
He follows through the starry night;
And with the early morning breeze,
Behold him on the azure seas.
The master of a trading dandy
Hires Robin for a go of brandy;
And all the happy hills of home
Vanish beyond the fields of foam.

Ben, meanwhile, like a tin reflector,
Attended on the worthy rector;
Opened his eyes and held his breath,
And flattered to the point of death;
And was at last, by that good fairy,
40   Apprenticed to the Apothecary.

So Ben, while Robin chose to roam,
A rising chemist was at home,
Tended his shop with learnèd air,
Watered his drugs and oiled his hair,
And gave advice to the unwary,
Like any sleek apothecary.

Meanwhile upon the deep afar
Robin the brave was waging war,
With other tarry desperadoes
50   About the latitude of Barbadoes.
He knew no touch of craven fear;
His voice was thunder in the cheer;
First, from the main-to'-gallan' high,
The skulking merchantman to spy –
The first to bound upon the deck,
The last to leave the sinking wreck.
His hand was steel, his word was law,
His mates regarded him with awe.
No pirate in the whole profession
60   Held a more honourable position.

At length, from years of anxious toil,
Bold Robin seeks his native soil;
Wisely arranges his affairs,
And to his native dale repairs.
The Bristol *Swallow* sets him down
Beside the well-remembered town.
He sighs, he spits, he marks the scene,
Proudly he treads the village green;
And free from pettiness and rancour,
70   Takes lodgings at the 'Crown and Anchor.'

Strange, when a man so great and good,
Once more in his home-country stood,
Strange that the sordid clowns should show
A dull desire to have him go.
His clinging breeks, his tarry hat,
The way he swore, the way he spat,
A certain quality of manner,
Alarming like the pirate's banner –
Something that did not seem to suit all –
80   Something, O call it bluff, not brutal –
Something at least, howe'er it's called,
Made Robin generally black-balled.

His soul was wounded; proud and glum,
Alone he sat and swigged his rum,
And took a great distaste to men
Till he encountered Chemist Ben.
Bright was the hour and bright the day,
That threw them in each other's way;
Glad were their mutual salutations,
90   Long their respective revelations.
Before the inn in sultry weather
They talked of this and that together;
Ben told the tale of his indentures,
And Rob narrated his adventures.
Last, as the point of greatest weight,
The pair contrasted their estate,
And Robin, like a boastful sailor,
Despised the other for a tailor.

'See,' he remarked, 'with envy, see
100 A man with such a fist as me!
Bearded and ringed, and big, and brown,
I sit and toss the stingo down,
Hear the gold jingle in my bag –
All won beneath the Jolly Flag!'

Ben moralised and shook his head:
'You wanderers earn and eat your bread.
The foe is found, beats or is beaten,
And either how, the wage is eaten.
And after all your pully-hauly
110   Your proceeds look uncommon small-ly.
You had done better here to tarry
Apprentice to the Apothecary.
The silent pirates of the shore
Eat and sleep soft, and pocket more
Than any red, robustious ranger
Who picks his farthings hot from danger.
You clank your guineas on the board;
Mine are with several bankers stored.
You reckon riches on your digits,
120   You dash in chase of Sals and Bridgets,
You drink and risk delirium tremens,
Your whole estate a common seaman's!
Regard your friend and school companion,
Soon to be wed to Miss Trevanion
(Smooth, honourable, fat and flowery,
With Heaven knows how much land in dowry).
Look at me – am I in good case?
Look at my hands, look at my face;
Look at the cloth of my apparel;
130   Try me and test me, lock and barrel;
And own, to give the devil his due,
I have made more of life than you.
Yet I nor sought nor risked a life;
I shudder at an open knife;
The perilous seas I still avoided
And stuck to land whate'er betided.
I had no gold, no marble quarry,
I was a poor apothecary,
Yet here I stand, at thirty-eight,
140   A man of an assured estate.'

'Well,' answered Robin – 'well, and how?'
The smiling chemist tapped his brow.
'Rob,' he replied, 'this throbbing brain
Still worked and hankered after gain.
By day and night, to work my will,
It pounded like a powder mill;
And marking how the world went round
A theory of theft it found.
Here is the key to right and wrong:
150   *Steal little, but steal all day long*;
And this invaluable plan
Marks what is called the Honest Man.
When first I served with Doctor Pill,
My hand was ever in the till.
Now that I am myself a master
My gains come softer still and faster.
As thus: on Wednesday, a maid
Came to me in the way of trade.
Her mother, an old farmer's wife,
160   Required a drug to save her life.
'At once, my dear, at once,' I said,
Patted the child upon the head,
Bade her be still a loving daughter,
And filled the bottle up with water.'

'Well, and the mother?' Robin cried.

'O she!' said Ben, 'I think she died.'

'Battle and blood, death and disease,
Upon the tainted Tropic seas –
The attendant sharks that chew the cud –
170   The abhorred scuppers spouting blood –
The untended dead, the Tropic sun –
The thunder of the murderous gun –

The cut-throat crew – the Captain's curse –
The tempest blustering worse and worse –
These have I known and these can stand,
But you, I settle out of hand!'

Out flashed the cutlass, down went Ben
Dead and rotten, there and then.

A CHILD'S GARDEN OF VERSES (1885)

To Alison Cunningham

From Her Boy

For the long nights you lay awake
And watched for my unworthy sake:
For your most comfortable hand
That led me through the uneven land:
For all the story-books you read:
For all the pains you comforted:
For all you pitied, all you bore,
In sad and happy days of yore:
My second Mother, my first Wife,
The angel of my infant life –
From the sick child, now well and old,
Take, nurse, the little book you hold!

And grant it, Heaven, that all who read
May find as dear a nurse at need,
And every child who lists my rhyme,
In the bright, fireside, nursery clime,
May hear it in as kind a voice
As made my childish days rejoice!

Bed in Summer

In winter I get up at night
And dress by yellow candle-light.
In summer, quite the other way,
I have to go to bed by day.

I have to go to bed and see
The birds still hopping on the tree,
Or hear the grown-up people's feet
Still going past me in the street.

And does it not seem hard to you,
10   When all the sky is clear and blue,
And I should like so much to play
To have to go to bed by day?

A Thought

It is very nice to think
The world is full of meat and drink,
With little children saying grace
In every Christian kind of place.

At the Seaside

When I was down beside the sea
A wooden spade they gave to me
    To dig the sandy shore.
My holes were empty like a cup,
In every hole the sea came up,
    Till it could come no more.

Young Night Thought

All night long and every night,
When my mamma puts out the light,
I see the people marching by,
As plain as day, before my eye.

Armies and emperors and kings,
All carrying different kinds of things,
And marching in so grand a way,
You never saw the like by day.

So fine a show was never seen,
10   At the great circus on the green;
For every kind of beast and man
Is marching in that caravan.

At first they move a little slow,
But still the faster on they go,
And still beside them close I keep
Until we reach the town of Sleep.

Whole Duty of Children

A child should always say what's true
And speak when he is spoken to,
And behave mannerly at table:
At least as far as he is able.

Rain

The rain is raining all around,
    It falls on field and tree,
It rains on the umbrellas here,
    And on the ships at sea.

Pirate Story

Three of us afloat in the meadow by the swing,
    Three of us aboard in the basket on the lea.
Winds are in the air, they are blowing in the spring,
    And waves are on the meadow like the waves there are at
        sea.

Where shall we adventure, to-day that we're afloat,
　　Wary of the weather and steering by a star?
Shall it be to Africa, a-steering of the boat,
　　To Providence, or Babylon, or off to Malabar?

Hi! but here's a squadron a-rowing on the sea –
10　　Cattle on the meadow a-charging with a roar!
Quick, and we'll escape them, they're as mad as they can be,
　　The wicket is the harbour and the garden is the shore.

Foreign Lands

Up into the cherry tree
Who should climb but little me?
I held the trunk with both my hands
And looked abroad on foreign lands.

I saw the next door garden lie,
Adorned with flowers, before my eye,
And many pleasant places more
That I had never seen before.

I saw the dimpling river pass
10　And be the sky's blue looking-glass;
The dusty roads go up and down
With people tramping in to town.

If I could find a higher tree
Farther and farther I should see,
To where the grown-up river slips
Into the sea among the ships,

To where the roads on either hand
Lead onward into fairy land,
Where all the children dine at five,
20　And all the playthings come alive.

Windy Nights

Whenever the moon and stars are set,
    Whenever the wind is high,
All night long in the dark and wet,
    A man goes riding by.
Late in the night when the fires are out,
Why does he gallop and gallop about?

Whenever the trees are crying aloud,
    And ships are tossed at sea,
By, on the highway, low and loud,
10   By at the gallop goes he.
By at the gallop he goes, and then
By he comes back at the gallop again.

Travel

I should like to rise and go
Where the golden apples grow;
Where below another sky
Parrot islands anchored lie,
And, watched by cockatoos and goats,
Lonely Crusoes building boats;
Where in sunshine reaching out
Eastern cities, miles about,
Are with mosque and minaret
10 Among sandy gardens set,
And the rich goods from near and far
Hang for sale in the bazaar;
Where the Great Wall round China goes,
And on one side the desert blows,
And with bell and voice and drum,
Cities on the other hum;
Where are forests, hot as fire,
Wide as England, tall as a spire,

Full of apes and cocoa-nuts
20   And the negro hunters' huts;
Where the knotty crocodile
Lies and blinks in the Nile,
And the red flamingo flies
Hunting fish before his eyes;
Where in jungles, near and far,
Man-devouring tigers are,
Lying close and giving ear
Lest the hunt be drawing near,
Or a comer-by be seen
30   Swinging in a palanquin;
Where among the desert sands
Some deserted city stands,
All its children, sweep and prince,
Grown to manhood ages since,
Not a foot in street or house,
Not a stir of child or mouse,
And when kindly falls the night,
In all the town no spark of light.
There I'll come when I'm a man
40   With a camel caravan;
Light a fire in the gloom
Of some dusty dining-room;
See the pictures on the walls,
Heroes, fights and festivals;
And in a corner find the toys
Of the old Egyptian boys.

Singing

Of speckled eggs the birdie sings
  And nests among the trees;
The sailor sings of ropes and things
  In ships upon the seas.

The children sing in far Japan,
   The children sing in Spain;
The organ with the organ man
   Is singing in the rain.

Looking Forward

When I am grown to man's estate
I shall be very proud and great.
And tell the other girls and boys
Not to meddle with my toys.

A Good Play

We built a ship upon the stairs
All made of the back-bedroom chairs,
And filled it full of sofa pillows
To go a-sailing on the billows.

We took a saw and several nails,
And water in the nursery pails;
And Tom said, 'Let us also take
An apple and a slice of cake';
Which was enough for Tom and me
To go a-sailing on, till tea.

We sailed along for days and days,
And had the very best of plays;
But Tom fell out and hurt his knee,
So there was no one left but me.

Where Go the Boats?

Dark brown is the river,
    Golden is the sand.
It flows along for ever,
    With trees on either hand.

Green leaves a-floating,
    Castles of the foam,
Boats of mine a-boating –
    Where will all come home?

On goes the river
10   And out past the mill,
Away down the valley,
    Away down the hill.

Away down the river,
    A hundred miles or more,
Other little children
    Shall bring my boats ashore.

Auntie's Skirts

Whenever Auntie moves around,
Her dresses make a curious sound;
They trail behind her up the floor,
And trundle after through the door.

The Land of Counterpane

When I was sick and lay a-bed,
I had two pillows at my head,
And all my toys beside me lay
To keep me happy all the day.

And sometimes for an hour or so
I watched my leaden soldiers go,
With different uniforms and drills,
Among the bed-clothes, through the hills;

And sometimes sent my ships in fleets
10   All up and down among the sheets;
Or brought my trees and houses out,
And planted cities all about.

I was the giant great and still
That sits upon the pillow-hill,
And sees before him, dale and plain,
The pleasant land of counterpane.

The Land of Nod

From breakfast on through all the day
At home among my friends I stay;
But every night I go abroad
Afar into the Land of Nod.

All by myself I have to go,
With none to tell me what to do –
All alone beside the streams
And up the mountain-sides of dreams.

The strangest things are there for me,
10   Both things to eat and things to see,
And many frightening sights abroad
Till morning in the Land of Nod.

Try as I like to find the way,
I never can get back by day,
Nor can remember plain and clear
The curious music that I hear.

My Shadow

I have a little shadow that goes in and out with me,
And what can be the use of him is more than I can see.
He is very, very like me from the heels up to the head;
And I see him jump before me, when I jump into my bed.

The funniest thing about him is the way he likes to grow –
Not at all like proper children, which is always very slow;
For he sometimes shoots up taller like an india-rubber ball,
And he sometimes gets so little that there's none of him
        at all.

He hasn't got a notion of how children ought to play,
And can only make a fool of me in every sort of way.
He stays so close beside me, he's a coward you can see;
I'd think shame to stick to nursie as that shadow sticks to me!

One morning, very early, before the sun was up,
I rose and found the shining dew on every buttercup;
But my lazy little shadow, like an arrant sleepy-head,
Had stayed at home behind me and was fast asleep in bed.

System

Every night my prayers I say,
And get my dinner every day;
And every day that I've been good,
I get an orange after food.

The child that is not clean and neat,
With lots of toys and things to eat,
He is a naughty child, I'm sure –
Or else his dear papa is poor.

A Good Boy

I woke before the morning, I was happy all the day,
I never said an ugly word, but smiled and stuck to play.

And now at last the sun is going down behind the wood,
And I am very happy, for I know that I've been good.

My bed is waiting cool and fresh, with linen smooth and fair,
And I must off to sleepsin-by, and not forget my prayer.

I know that, till to-morrow I shall see the sun arise,
No ugly dream shall fright my mind, no ugly sight my eyes,

But slumber hold me tightly till I waken in the dawn,
10   And hear the thrushes singing in the lilacs round the lawn.

Escape at Bedtime

The lights from the parlour and kitchen shone out
    Through the blinds and the windows and bars;
And high overhead and all moving about,
    There were thousands of millions of stars.
There ne'er were such thousands of leaves on a tree,
    Nor of people in church or the Park,
As the crowds of the stars that looked down upon me,
    And that glittered and winked in the dark.

The Dog, and the Plough, and the Hunter, and all,
10   And the star of the sailor, and Mars,
These shone in the sky, and the pail by the wall
    Would be half full of water and stars.
They saw me at last, and they chased me with cries,
    And they soon had me packed into bed;
But the glory kept shining and bright in my eyes,
    And the stars going round in my head.

Marching Song

Bring the comb and play upon it!
    Marching, here we come!
Willie cocks his highland bonnet,
    Johnnie beats the drum.

Mary Jane commands the party,
    Peter leads the rear;
Feet in time, alert and hearty,
    Each a Grenadier!

All in the most martial manner
10   Marching double-quick;
While the napkin like a banner
    Waves upon the stick!

Here's enough of fame and pillage,
    Great commander Jane!
Now that we've been round the village,
    Let's go home again.

The Cow

The friendly cow all red and white,
    I love with all my heart:
She gives me cream with all her might,
    To eat with apple-tart.

She wanders lowing here and there,
    And yet she cannot stray,
All in the pleasant open air,
    The pleasant light of day;

And blown by all the winds that pass
10   And wet with all the showers,
She walks among the meadow grass
        And eats the meadow flowers.

Happy Thought

The world is so full of a number of things,
I'm sure we should all be as happy as kings.

The Wind

I saw you toss the kites on high
And blow the birds about the sky;
And all around I heard you pass,
Like ladies' skirts across the grass –
        O wind, a-blowing all day long,
        O wind, that sings so loud a song!

I saw the different things you did,
But always you yourself you hid.
I felt you push, I heard you call,
10 I could not see yourself at all –
        O wind, a-blowing all day long,
        O wind, that sings so loud a song!

O you that are so strong and cold,
O blower, are you young or old?
Are you a beast of field and tree,
Or just a stronger child than me?
        O wind, a-blowing all day long,
        O wind, that sings so loud a song!

Keepsake Mill

Over the borders, a sin without pardon,
  Breaking the branches and crawling below,
Out through the breach in the wall of the garden,
  Down by the banks of the river, we go.

Here is the mill with the humming of thunder,
  Here is the weir with the wonder of foam,
Here is the sluice with the race running under –
  Marvellous places, though handy to home!

Sounds of the village grow stiller and stiller,
10   Stiller the note of the birds on the hill;
Dusty and dim are the eyes of the miller,
  Deaf are his ears with the moil of the mill.

Years may go by, and the wheel in the river
  Wheel as it wheels for us, children, today,
Wheel and keep roaring and foaming for ever
  Long after all of the boys are away.

Home from the Indies and home from the ocean,
  Heroes and soldiers we all shall come home;
Still we shall find the old mill wheel in motion,
20   Turning and churning that river to foam.

You with the bean that I gave when we quarrelled,
  I with your marble of Saturday last,
Honoured and old and all gaily apparelled,
  Here we shall meet and remember the past.

Good and Bad Children

Children, you are very little,
And your bones are very brittle;
If you would grow great and stately,
You must try to walk sedately.

You must still be bright and quiet,
And content with simple diet;
And remain, through all bewild'ring,
Innocent and honest children.

Happy hearts and happy faces,
10   Happy play in grassy places –
That was how, in ancient ages,
Children grew to kings and sages.

But the unkind and the unruly,
And the sort who eat unduly,
They must never hope for glory –
Theirs is quite a different story!

Cruel children, crying babies,
All grow up as geese and gabies,
Hated, as their age increases,
20   By their nephews and their nieces.

Foreign Children

Little Indian, Sioux or Crow,
Little frosty Eskimo,
Little Turk or Japanee,
O! don't you wish that you were me?

You have seen the scarlet trees
And the lions over seas;
You have eaten ostrich eggs,
And turned the turtles off their legs.

Such a life is very fine,
10   But it's not so nice as mine:
You must often, as you trod,
Have wearied *not* to be abroad.

You have curious things to eat,
I am fed on proper meat;
You must dwell beyond the foam,
But I am safe and live at home.

Little Indian, Sioux or Crow,
Little frosty Eskimo,
Little Turk or Japanee,
20   O! don't you wish that you were me?

The Sun's Travels

The sun is not a-bed, when I
At night upon my pillow lie;
Still round the earth his way he takes,
And morning after morning makes.

While here at home, in shining day,
We round the sunny garden play,
Each little Indian sleepy-head
Is being kissed and put to bed.

And when at eve I rise from tea,
10   Day dawns beyond the Atlantic Sea,
And all the children in the West
Are getting up and being dressed.

The Lamplighter

My tea is nearly ready and the sun has left the sky;
It's time to take the window to see Leerie going by;
For every night at teatime and before you take your seat,
With lantern and with ladder he comes posting up the street.

Now Tom would be a driver and Maria go to sea,
And my papa's a banker and as rich as he can be;
But I, when I am stronger and can choose what I'm to do,
O Leerie, I'll go round at night and light the lamps with you!

For we are very lucky, with a lamp before the door,
And Leerie stops to light it as he lights so many more;
And O! before you hurry by with ladder and with light,
O Leerie, see a little child and nod to him to-night!

My Bed is a Boat

My bed is like a little boat;
   Nurse helps me in when I embark;
She girds me in my sailor's coat
   And starts me in the dark.

At night, I go on board and say
   Good-night to all my friends on shore;
I shut my eyes and sail away
   And see and hear no more.

And sometimes things to bed I take,
   As prudent sailors have to do:
Perhaps a slice of wedding-cake,
   Perhaps a toy or two.

All night across the dark we steer:
   But when the day returns at last,
Safe in my room, beside the pier,
   I find my vessel fast.

The Moon

The moon has a face like the clock in the hall;
She shines on thieves on the garden wall,
On streets and fields and harbour quays,
And birdies asleep in the forks of the trees.

The squalling cat and the squeaking mouse,
The howling dog by the door of the house,
The bat that lies in bed at noon,
All love to be out by the light of the moon.

But all of the things that belong to the day
10 Cuddle to sleep to be out of her way;
And flowers and children close their eyes
Till up in the morning the sun shall arise.

The Swing

How do you like to go up in a swing,
   Up in the air so blue?
Oh, I do think it the pleasantest thing
   Ever a child can do!

Up in the air and over the wall,
   Till I can see so wide,
Rivers and trees and cattle and all
   Over the countryside –

Till I look down on the garden green,
10   Down on the roof so brown –
Up in the air I go flying again,
    Up in the air and down!

Time to Rise

A birdie with a yellow bill
Hopped upon the window sill,
Cocked his shining eye and said:
'Ain't you 'shamed, you sleepy-head?'

Looking-Glass River

Smooth it slides upon its travel,
    Here a wimple, there a gleam –
        O the clean gravel!
        O the smooth stream!

Sailing blossoms, silver fishes,
    Paven pools as clear as air –
        How a child wishes
        To live down there!

We can see our coloured faces
10   Floating on the shaken pool
        Down in cool places,
        Dim and very cool;

Till a wind or water wrinkle,
    Dipping marten, plumping trout,
        Spreads in a twinkle
        And blots all out.

See the rings pursue each other;
   All below grows black as night,
     Just as if mother
20   Had blown out the light!

Patience, children, just a minute –
   See the spreading circles die;
     The stream and all in it
     Will clear by-and-by.

Fairy-Bread

Come up here, O dusty feet!
   Here is fairy-bread to eat.
Here in my retiring room,
   Children, you may dine
On the golden smell of broom
   And the shade of pine;
And when you have eaten well,
Fairy stories hear and tell.

From a Railway Carriage

Faster than fairies, faster than witches,
Bridges and houses, hedges and ditches;
And charging along like troops in a battle,
All through the meadows the horses and cattle:
All of the sights of the hill and the plain
Fly as thick as driving rain;
And ever again, in the wink of an eye,
Painted stations whistle by.

Here is a child who clambers and scrambles,
All by himself and gathering brambles;
Here is a tramp who stands and gazes;
And there is the green for stringing the daisies!
Here is a cart run away in the road
Lumping along with man and load;
And here is a mill and there is a river:
Each a glimpse and gone for ever!

Winter Time

Late lies the wintry sun a-bed,
A frosty, fiery sleepy-head;
Blinks but an hour or two; and then,
A blood-red orange, sets again.

Before the stars have left the skies,
At morning in the dark I rise;
And shivering in my nakedness,
By the cold candle, bathe and dress.

Close by the jolly fire I sit
To warm my frozen bones a bit;
Or with a reindeer-sled, explore
The colder countries round the door.

When to go out, my nurse doth wrap
Me in my comforter and cap:
The cold wind burns my face, and blows
Its frosty pepper up my nose.

Black are my steps on silver sod;
Thick blows my frosty breath abroad;
And tree and house, and hill and lake,
Are frosted like a wedding-cake.

The Hayloft

Through all the pleasant meadow-side
    The grass grew shoulder-high,
Till the shining scythes went far and wide
    And cut it down to dry.

These green and sweetly smelling crops
    They led in waggons home;
And they piled them here in mountain tops
    For mountaineers to roam.

Here is Mount Clear, Mount Rusty-Nail,
10   Mount Eagle and Mount High;
The mice that in these mountains dwell,
    No happier are than I!

O what a joy to clamber there,
    O what a place for play,
With the sweet, the dim, the dusty air,
    The happy hills of hay!

Farewell to the Farm

The coach is at the door at last;
The eager children, mounting fast
And kissing hands, in chorus sing:
Good-bye, good-bye, to everything!

To house and garden, field and lawn,
The meadow-gates we swang upon,
To pump and stable, tree and swing,
Good-bye, good-bye, to everything!

And fare you well for evermore,
10   O ladder at the hayloft door,
O hayloft where the cobwebs cling,
Good-bye, good-bye, to everything!

Crack goes the whip, and off we go;
The trees and houses smaller grow;
Last, round the woody turn we swing:
Good-bye, good-bye, to everything!

North-West Passage

I GOOD NIGHT

When the bright lamp is carried in,
The sunless hours again begin;
O'er all without, in field and lane,
The haunted night returns again.

Now we behold the embers flee
About the firelit hearth; and see
Our faces painted as we pass,
Like pictures, on the window-glass.

Must we to bed indeed? Well then,
10   Let us arise and go like men,
And face with an undaunted tread
The long black passage up to bed.

Farewell, O brother, sister, sire!
O pleasant party round the fire?
The songs you sing, the tales you tell,
Till far to-morrow, fare ye well!

II SHADOW MARCH
All round the house is the jet-black night;
    It stares through the window-pane;
It crawls in the corners, hiding from the light,
20   And it moves with the moving flame.

Now my little heart goes a-beating like a drum,
    With the breath of the Bogie in my hair;
And all round the candle the crooked shadows come
    And go marching along up the stair.

The shadow of the balusters, the shadow of the lamp,
    The shadow of the child that goes to bed –
All the wicked shadows coming, tramp, tramp, tramp,
    With the black night overhead.

III IN PORT
Last, to the chamber where I lie
30 My fearful footsteps patter nigh,
And come from out the cold and gloom
Into my warm and cheerful room.

There, safe arrived, we turn about
To keep the coming shadows out,
And close the happy door at last
On all the perils that we past.

Then, when mamma goes by to bed,
She shall come in with tip-toe tread,
And see me lying warm and fast
40 And in the Land of Nod at last.

THE CHILD ALONE

The Unseen Playmate

When children are playing alone on the green,
In comes the playmate that never was seen.
When children are happy and lonely and good,
The Friend of the Children comes out of the wood.

Nobody heard him and nobody saw,
His is a picture you never could draw
But he's sure to be present, abroad or at home,
When children are happy and playing alone.

He lies in the laurels, he runs on the grass,
10   He sings when you tinkle the musical glass;
Whene'er you are happy and cannot tell why,
The Friend of the Children is sure to be by!

He loves to be little, he hates to be big,
'Tis he that inhabits the caves that you dig;
'Tis he when you play with your soldiers of tin
That sides with the Frenchmen and never can win.

'Tis he, when at night you go off to your bed,
Bids you go to your sleep and not trouble your head;
For wherever they're lying, in cupboard or shelf,
20   'Tis he will take care of your playthings himself!

My Ship and I

O it's I that am the captain of a tidy little ship,
    Of a ship that goes a-sailing on the pond;
And my ship it keeps a-turning all around and all about;
But when I'm a little older, I shall find the secret out
    How to send my vessel sailing on beyond.

For I mean to grow as little as the dolly at the helm,
    And the dolly I intend to come alive;
And with him beside to help me, it's a-sailing I shall go,
It's a-sailing on the water, when the jolly breezes blow,
10   And the vessel goes a divie-divie-dive.

O it's then you'll see me sailing through the rushes and the
        reeds,
    And you'll hear the water singing at the prow;
For beside the dolly sailor, I'm to voyage and explore,
        To land upon the island where no dolly was before,
        And to fire the penny cannon in the bow.

My Kingdom

Down by a shining water well
I found a very little dell,
    No higher than my head.
The heather and the gorse about
In summer bloom were coming out,
    Some yellow and some red.

I called the little pool a sea;
The little hills were big to me;
    For I am very small.
10 I made a boat, I made a town,
I searched the caverns up and down,
    And named them one and all.

And all about was mine, I said,
The little sparrows overhead,
 The little minnows too.
This was the world and I was king;
For me the bees came by to sing,
 For me the swallows flew.

I played there were no deeper seas,
20 Nor any wider plains than these,
  Nor other kings than me.
At last I heard my mother call
Out from the house at evenfall,
 To call me home to tea.

And I must rise and leave my dell,
And leave my dimpled water well,
 And leave my heather blooms.
Alas! and as my home I neared,
How very big my nurse appeared,
30 How great and cool the rooms!

Picture Books in Winter

Summer fading, winter comes –
Frosty mornings, tingling thumbs,
Window robins, winter rooks,
And the picture story-books.

Water now is turned to stone
Nurse and I can walk upon;
Still we find the flowing brooks
In the picture story-books.

All the pretty things put by,
10 Wait upon the children's eye,
Sheep and shepherds, trees and crooks,
In the picture story-books.

We may see how all things are,
Seas and cities, near and far,
And the flying fairies' looks,
In the picture story-books.

How am I to sing your praise,
Happy chimney-corner days,
Sitting safe in nursery nooks,
20   Reading picture story-books?

My Treasures

These nuts, that I keep in the back of the nest
Where all my lead soldiers are lying at rest,
Were gathered in autumn by nursie and me
In a wood with a well by the side of the sea.

This whistle we made (and how clearly it sounds!)
By the side of a field at the end of the grounds,
Of a branch of a plane, with a knife of my own,
It was nursie who made it, and nursie alone!

The stone, with the white and the yellow and grey,
10   We discovered I cannot tell *how* far away;
And I carried it back although weary and cold,
For though father denies it, I'm sure it is gold.

But of all of my treasures the last is the king,
For there's very few children possess such a thing;
And that is a chisel, both handle and blade,
Which a man who was really a carpenter made.

Block City

What are you able to build with your blocks?
Castles and palaces, temples and docks.
Rain may keep raining, and others go roam,
But I can be happy and building at home.

Let the sofa be mountains, the carpet be sea,
There I'll establish a city for me:
A kirk and a mill and a palace beside,
And a harbour as well where my vessels may ride.

Great is the palace with pillar and wall,
A sort of a tower on the top of it all,
And steps coming down in an orderly way
To where my toy vessels lie safe in the bay.

This one is sailing and that one is moored:
Hark to the song of the sailors on board!
And see on the steps of my palace, the kings
Coming and going with presents and things!

Now I have done with it, down let it go!
All in a moment the town is laid low.
Block upon block lying scattered and free,
What is there left of my town by the sea?

Yet as I saw it, I see it again,
The kirk and the palace, the ships and the men,
And as long as I live and where'er I may be,
I'll always remember my town by the sea.

The Land of Story-Books

At evening, when the lamp is lit,
Around the fire my parents sit;
They sit at home and talk and sing,
And do not play at anything.

Now, with my little gun, I crawl
All in the dark along the wall,
And follow round the forest track
Away behind the sofa back.

There, in the night, where none can spy,
All in my hunter's camp I lie,
And play at books that I have read
Till it is time to go to bed.

These are the hills, these are the woods,
These are my starry solitudes;
And there the river by whose brink
The roaring lions come to drink.

I see the others far away
As if in firelit camp they lay,
And I, like to an Indian scout,
Around their party prowled about.

So, when my nurse comes in for me,
Home I return across the sea,
And go to bed with backward looks
At my dear land of Story-books.

Armies in the Fire

The lamps now glitter down the street;
Faintly sound the falling feet;
And the blue even slowly falls
About the garden trees and walls.

Now in the falling of the gloom
The red fire paints the empty room:
And warmly on the roof it looks,
And flickers on the backs of books.

Armies march by tower and spire
10   Of cities blazing, in the fire;
Till as I gaze with staring eyes,
The armies fade, the lustre dies.

Then once again the glow returns;
Again the phantom city burns;
And down the red-hot valley, lo!
The phantom armies marching go!

Blinking embers, tell me true
Where are those armies marching to,
And what the burning city is
20   That crumbles in your furnaces!

The Little Land

When at home alone I sit
And am very tired of it,
I have just to shut my eyes
To go sailing through the skies –
To go sailing far away
To the pleasant Land of Play;

To the fairy land afar
Where the Little People are;
Where the clover-tops are trees,
And the rain-pools are the seas,
And the leaves like little ships
Sail about on tiny trips;
And above the daisy tree
    Through the grasses,
High o'erhead the Bumble Bee
    Hums and passes.

In that forest to and fro
I can wander, I can go;
See the spider and the fly,
And the ants go marching by
Carrying parcels with their feet
Down the green and grassy street.
I can in the sorrel sit
Where the ladybird alit.
I can climb the jointed grass;
    And on high
See the greater swallows pass
    In the sky,
And the round sun rolling by
Heeding no such things as I.

Through that forest I can pass
Till, as in a looking-glass,
Humming fly and daisy tree
And my tiny self I see,
Painted very clear and neat
On the rain-pool at my feet.
Should a leaflet come to land
Drifting near to where I stand,
Straight I'll board that tiny boat
Round the rain-pool sea to float.

Little thoughtful creatures sit
On the grassy coasts of it;
Little things with lovely eyes
See me sailing with surprise.
Some are clad in armour green –
(These have sure to battle been!) –
Some are pied with ev'ry hue,
Black and crimson, gold and blue;
Some have wings and swift are gone;
50 But they all look kindly on.

When my eyes I once again
Open, and see all things plain:
High bare walls, great bare floor;
Great big knobs on drawer and door;
Great big people perched on chairs,
Stitching tucks and mending tears,
Each a hill that I could climb,
And talking nonsense all the time –
        O dear me,
60   That I could be
A sailor on the rain-pool sea,
A climber in the clover tree,
And just come back, a sleepy head.
Late at night to go to bed.

GARDEN DAYS

Night and Day

When the golden day is done,
    Through the closing portal,
Child and garden, flower and sun,
    Vanish all things mortal.

As the blinding shadows fall,
    As the rays diminish,
Under evening's cloak, they all
    Roll away and vanish.

Garden darkened, daisy shut,
10   Child in bed, they slumber –
Glow-worm in the highway rut,
    Mice among the lumber.

In the darkness houses shine,
    Parents move with candles;
Till on all, the night divine
    Turns the bedroom handles.

Till at last the day begins
    In the east a-breaking,
In the hedges and the whins
20   Sleeping birds a-waking.

In the darkness shapes of things,
    Houses, trees, and hedges,
Clearer grow; and sparrow's wings
    Beat on window ledges.

These shall wake the yawning maid;
    She the door shall open –
Finding dew on garden glade
    And the morning broken.

There my garden grows again
30   Green and rosy painted,
As at eve behind the pane
    From my eyes it fainted.

Just as it was shut away,
    Toy-like, in the even,
Here I see it glow with day
    Under glowing heaven.

Every path and every plot,
  Every bush of roses,
Every blue forget-me-not
40   Where the dew reposes,

'Up!' they cry, 'the day is come
  On the smiling valleys:
We have beat the morning drum;
  Playmate, join your allies!'

Nest Eggs

Birds all the sunny day
  Flutter and quarrel
Here in the arbour-like
  Tent of the laurel.

Here in the fork
  The brown nest is seated;
Four little blue eggs
  The mother keeps heated.

While we stand watching her,
10   Staring like gabies,
Safe in each egg are the
  Birds' little babies.

Soon the frail eggs they shall
  Chip, and upspringing
Make all the April woods
  Merry with singing.

Younger than we are,
  O children, and frailer,
Soon in blue air they'll be.
20   Singer and sailor.

We, so much older,
   Taller and stronger,
We shall look down on the
   Birdies no longer.

They shall go flying
   With musical speeches
High overhead in the
   Tops of the beeches.

In spite of our wisdom
30   And sensible talking,
We on our feet must go
   Plodding and walking.

The Flowers

All the names I know from nurse:
Gardener's garters, Shepherd's purse,
Bachelor's buttons, Lady's smock,
And the Lady Hollyhock.

Fairy places, fairy things,
Fairy woods where the wild bee wings,
Tiny trees for tiny dames –
These must all be fairy names!

Tiny woods below whose boughs
10   Shady fairies weave a house;
Tiny tree tops, rose or thyme,
Where the braver fairies climb!

Fair are grown-up people's trees,
But the fairest woods are these;
Where if I were not so tall,
I should live for good and all.

Summer Sun

Great is the sun, and wide he goes
Through empty heaven without repose;
And in the blue and glowing days
More thick than rain he showers his rays.

Though closer still the blinds we pull
To keep the shady parlour cool,
Yet he will find a chink or two
To slip his golden fingers through.

The dusty attic spider-clad
10 He, through the keyhole, maketh glad;
And through the broken edge of tiles,
Into the laddered hayloft smiles.

Meantime his golden face around
He bares to all the garden ground,
And sheds a warm and glittering look
Among the ivy's inmost nook.

Above the hills, along the blue,
Round the bright air with footing true,
To please the child, to paint the rose,
20 The gardener of the World, he goes.

The Dumb Soldier

When the grass was closely mown,
Walking on the lawn alone,
In the turf a hole I found
And hid a soldier underground.

Spring and daisies came apace;
Grasses hide my hiding place;
Grasses run like a green sea
O'er the lawn up to my knee.

Under grass alone he lies,
10   Looking up with leaden eyes,
Scarlet coat and pointed gun,
To the stars and to the sun.

When the grass is ripe like grain,
When the scythe is stoned again,
When the lawn is shaven clear,
Then my hole shall reappear.

I shall find him, never fear,
I shall find my grenadier;
But for all that's gone and come,
20   I shall find my soldier dumb.

He has lived, a little thing,
In the grassy woods of spring;
Done, if he could tell me true,
Just as I should like to do.

He has seen the starry hours
And the springing of the flowers;
And the fairy things that pass
In the forests of the grass.

In the silence he has heard
30   Talking bee and ladybird,
And the butterfly has flown
O'er him as he lay alone.

Not a word will he disclose,
Not a word of all he knows.
I must lay him on the shelf,
And make up the tale myself.

Autumn Fires

In the other gardens
    And all up the vale,
From the autumn bonfires
    See the smoke trail!

Pleasant summer over
    And all the summer flowers,
The red fire blazes,
    The grey smoke towers.

Sing a song of seasons!
10   Something bright in all!
Flowers in the summer,
    Fires in the fall!

The Gardener

The gardener does not love to talk,
He makes me keep the gravel walk;
And when he puts his tools away,
He locks the door and takes the key.

Away behind the currant row
Where no one else but cook may go,
Far in the plots, I see him dig
Old and serious, brown and big.

He digs the flowers, green, red and blue,
10 Nor wishes to be spoken to.
He digs the flowers and cuts the hay,
And never seems to want to play.

Silly gardener! summer goes,
And winter comes with pinching toes,

When in the garden bare and brown
You must lay your barrow down.

Well now, and while the summer stays
To profit by these garden days
O how much wiser you would be
20   To play at Indian wars with me!

Historical Associations

Dear Uncle Jim, this garden ground
That now you smoke your pipe around,
Has seen immortal actions done
And valiant battles lost and won.

Here we had best on tip-toe tread,
While I for safety march ahead,
For this is that enchanted ground
Where all who loiter slumber sound.

Here is the sea, here is the sand,
10   Here is simple Shepherd's Land,
Here are the fairy hollyhocks,
And there are Ali Baba's rocks.

But yonder, see! apart and high,
Frozen Siberia lies; where I,
With Robert Bruce and William Tell,
Was bound by an enchanter's spell.

There, then, awhile in chains we lay,
In wintry dungeons, far from day;
But ris'n at length, with might and main,
20   Our iron fetters burst in twain.

Then all the horns were blown in town;
And to the ramparts clanging down,
All the giants leaped to horse
And charged behind us through the gorse.

On we rode, the others and I,
Over the mountains blue, and by
The Silver River, the sounding sea
And the robber woods of Tartary.

30
A thousand miles we galloped fast,
And down the witches' lane we passed,
And rode amain, with brandished sword,
Up to the middle, through the ford.

Last we drew rein – a weary three –
Upon the lawn, in time for tea,
And from our steeds alighted down
Before the gates of Babylon.

ENVOYS

To Willie and Henrietta

If two may read aright
These rhymes of old delight
And house and garden play,
You two, my cousins, and you only, may.

You in a garden green
With me were king and queen,
Were hunter, soldier, tar,
And all the thousand things that children are.

Now in the elders' seat

10   We rest with quiet feet,
And from the window-bay
We watch the children, our successors, play.

'Time was,' the golden head
Irrevocably said;
But time which none can bind,
While flowing fast away, leaves love behind.

To My Mother

You too, my mother, read my rhymes
For love of unforgotten times,
And you may chance to hear once more
The little feet along the floor.

To Auntie

Chief of our aunts – not only I,
But all your dozen of nurslings cry –
What did the other children do?
And what were childhood, wanting you?

To Minnie

The red room with the giant bed
Where none but elders laid their head;
The little room where you and I
Did for awhile together lie
And, simple suitor, I your hand
In decent marriage did demand;
The great day nursery, best of all,
With pictures pasted on the wall

And leaves upon the blind –
10 A pleasant room wherein to wake
And hear the leafy garden shake
And rustle in the wind –
And pleasant there to lie in bed
And see the pictures overhead –
The wars about Sebastopol,
The grinning guns along the wall,
The daring escalade,
The plunging ships, the bleating sheep,
The happy children ankle-deep
20 And laughing as they wade:
All these are vanished clean away,
And the old manse is changed today;
It wears an altered face
And shields a stranger race.

The river, on from mill to mill,
Flows past our childhood's garden still;
But ah! we children never more
Shall watch it from the water-door!
Below the yew – it still is there –
30 Our phantom voices haunt the air
As we were still at play,
And I can hear them call and say:
'*How far is it to Babylon?*'

Ah, far enough, my dear,
Far, far enough from here –
Yet you have farther gone!
'*Can I get there by candlelight?*'
So goes the old refrain.
I do not know – perchance you might –
40 But only, children, hear it right,
Ah, never to return again!
The eternal dawn, beyond a doubt,
Shall break on hill and plain,
And put all stars and candles out,
Ere we be young again.

To you in distant India, these
I send across the seas,
Nor count it far across.
For which of us forgets
50   The Indian cabinets,
The bones of antelope, the wings of albatross,
The pied and painted birds and beans,
The junks and bangles, beads and screens,
The gods and sacred bells,
And the loud-humming, twisted shells?
The level of the parlour floor
Was honest, homely, Scottish shore;
But when we climbed upon a chair,
Behold the gorgeous East was there!
60   Be this a fable; and behold
Me in the parlour as of old,
And Minnie just above me set
In the quaint Indian cabinet!
Smiling and kind, you grace a shelf
Too high for me to reach myself.
Reach down a hand, my dear, and take
These rhymes for old acquaintance' sake.

To My Name-Child

I

Some day soon this rhyming volume, if you learn with proper
        speed,
Little Louis Sanchez, will be given you to read.
Then shall you discover that your name was printed down
By the English printers, long before, in London town.

In the great and busy city where the East and West are met,
All the little letters did the English printer set;
While you thought of nothing, and were still too young
        to play,
Foreign people thought of you in places far away.

Ay, and while you slept, a baby, over all the English lands
10   Other little children took the volume in their hands;
Other children questioned, in their homes across the seas:
Who was little Louis, won't you tell us, mother, please?

II
Now that you have spelt your lesson, lay it down and go
        and play,
Seeking shells and seaweed on the sands of Monterey,
Watching all the mighty whalebones, lying buried by
        the breeze,
Tiny sandy-pipers, and the huge Pacific seas.

And remember in your playing, as the sea-fog rolls to you,
Long ere you could read it, how I told you what to do;
And that while you thought of no one, nearly half the
        world away
20   Some one thought of Louis on the beach of Monterey!

To Any Reader

As from the house your mother sees
You playing round the garden trees,
So you may see, if you will look
Through the windows of this book,
Another child, far, far away,
And in another garden, play.
But do not think you can at all,
By knocking on the window, call
That child to hear you. He intent
10   Is all on his play-business bent.
He does not hear; he will not look,
Nor yet be lured out of this book.
For, long ago, the truth to say,
He has grown up and gone away,
And it is but a child of air
That lingers in the garden there.

FROM *UNDERWOODS* (1887)

BOOK ONE

I Envoy

Go, little book, and wish to all
Flowers in the garden, meat in the hall,
A bin of wine, a spice of wit,
A house with lawns enclosing it,
A living river by the door,
A nightingale in the sycamore!

III The Canoe Speaks

On the great streams the ships may go
About men's business to and fro.
But I, the egg-shell pinnace, sleep
On crystal waters ankle-deep:
I, whose diminutive design,
Of sweeter cedar, pithier pine,
Is fashioned on so frail a mould,
A hand may launch, a hand withhold:
I, rather, with the leaping trout
Wind, among lilies, in and out;
I, the unnamed, inviolate,
Green, rustic rivers, navigate;
My dipping paddle scarcely shakes
The berry in the bramble-brakes;
Still forth on my green way I wend
Beside the cottage garden-end;
And by the nested angler fare,
And take the lovers unaware.
By willow wood and water-wheel
Speedily fleets my touching keel;
By all retired and shady spots
Where prosper dim forget-me-nots;

By meadows where at afternoon
The growing maidens troop in June
To loose their girdles on the grass.
Ah! speedier than before the glass
The backward toilet goes; and swift
As swallows quiver, robe and shift
And the rough country stockings lie
30   Around each young divinity.
When, following the recondite brook,
Sudden upon this scene I look,
And light with unfamiliar face
On chaste Diana's bathing-place,
Loud ring the hills about and all
The shallows are abandoned. . . .

V The House Beautiful

A naked house, a naked moor,
A shivering pool before the door,
A garden bare of flowers and fruit
And poplars at the garden foot:
Such is the place that I live in,
Bleak without and bare within.

Yet shall your ragged moor receive
The incomparable pomp of eve,
And the cold glories of the dawn
10   Behind your shivering trees be drawn;
And when the wind from place to place
Doth the unmoored cloud-galleons chase,
Your garden gloom and gleam again,
With leaping sun, with glancing rain.
Here shall the wizard moon ascend
The heavens, in the crimson end
Of day's declining splendour; here
The army of the stars appear.

The neighbour hollows dry or wet,
20   Spring shall with tender flowers beset;
And oft the morning muser see
Larks rising from the broomy lea,
And ever fairy wheel and thread
Of cobweb dew-bediamonded.
When daisies go, shall winter time
Silver the simple grass with rime;
Autumnal frosts enchant the pool
And make the cart-ruts beautiful;
And when snow-bright the moor expands,
30   How shall your children clap their hands!
To make this earth, our hermitage,
A cheerful and a changeful page,
God's bright and intricate device
Of days and seasons doth suffice.

VI *To a Gardener*

Friend, in my mountain-side demesne,
My plain-beholding, rosy, green
And linnet-haunted garden-ground,
Let still the esculents abound.
Let first the onion flourish there,
Rose among roots, the maiden-fair,
Wine-scented and poetic soul
Of the capacious salad bowl.
Let thyme the mountaineer (to dress
10   The tinier birds) and wading cress,
The lover of the shallow brook,
For all my plots and borders look.
Nor crisp and ruddy radish, nor
Pease-cods for the child's pinafore
Be lacking; nor of salad clan
The last and least that ever ran
About great nature's garden-beds.
Nor thence be missed the speary heads

Of artichoke; nor thence the bean
20   That gathered innocent and green
Outsavours the belauded pea.

These tend, I prithee; and for me,
Thy most long-suffering master, bring
In April, when the linnets sing
And the days lengthen more and more
At sundown to the garden door.
And I, being provided thus,
Shall, with superb asparagus,
A book, a taper, and a cup
30   Of country wine, divinely sup.

IX *To K. de M.*

A lover of the moorland bare
And honest country winds, you were;
The silver-skimming rain you took;
And loved the floodings of the brook,
Dew, frost and mountains, fire and seas,
Tumultuary silences,
Winds that in darkness fifed a tune,
And the high-riding, virgin moon.

And as the berry, pale and sharp,
10   Springs on some ditch's counterscarp
In our ungenial, native north –
You put your frosted wildings forth,
And on the heath, afar from man,
A strong and bitter virgin ran.

The berry ripened keeps the rude
And racy flavour of the wood.
And you that loved the empty plain
All redolent of wind and rain,

Around you still the curlew sings –
20 The freshness of the weather clings –
The maiden jewels of the rain
Sit in your dabbled locks again.

X *To N. V. de G. S.*

The unfathomable sea, and time, and tears,
The deeds of heroes and the crimes of kings
Dispart us; and the river of events
Has, for an age of years, to east and west
More widely borne our cradles. Thou to me
Art foreign, as when seamen at the dawn
Descry a land far off and know not which.
So I approach uncertain; so I cruise
Round thy mysterious islet, and behold
10 Surf and great mountains and loud river-bars,
And from the shore hear inland voices call.
Strange is the seaman's heart; he hopes, he fears;
Draws closer and sweeps wider from that coast;
Last, his rent sail refits, and to the deep
His shattered prow uncomforted puts back.
Yet as he goes he ponders at the helm
Of that bright island; where he feared to touch,
His spirit rëadventures; and for years,
Where by his wife he slumbers safe at home,
20 Thoughts of that land revisit him; he sees
The eternal mountains beckon, and awakes
Yearning for that far home that might have been.

XII *To Mrs Will H. Low*

Even in the bluest noonday of July,
There could not run the smallest breath of wind
But all the quarter sounded like a wood;
And in the chequered silence and above
The hum of city cabs that sought the Bois,
Suburban ashes shivered into song.
A patter and a chatter and a chirp
And a long dying hiss – it was as though
Starched old brocaded dames through all the house
10 Had trailed a strident skirt, or the whole sky
Even in a wink had over-brimmed in rain.
Hark, in these shady parlours, how it talks
Of the near Autumn, how the smitten ash
Trembles and augurs floods! O not too long
In these inconstant latitudes delay,
O not too late from the unbeloved north
Trim your escape! For soon shall this low roof
Resound indeed with rain, soon shall your eyes
Search the foul garden, search the darkened rooms,
20 Nor find one jewel but the blazing log.

XIII *To H. F. Brown*

Written during a dangerous sickness

I sit and wait a pair of oars
On cis-Elysian river-shores.
Where the immortal dead have sate,
'Tis mine to sit and meditate;
To re-ascend life's rivulet,
Without remorse, without regret;
And sing my *Alma Genetrix*
Among the willows of the Styx.

And lo, as my serener soul
10 Did these unhappy shores patrol,
And wait with an attentive ear
The coming of the gondolier,
Your fire-surviving roll I took,
Your spirited and happy book;
Whereon, despite my frowning fate,
It did my soul so recreate
That all my fancies fled away
On a Venetian holiday.

Now, thanks to your triumphant care,
20 Your pages clear as April air,
The sails, the bells, the birds, I know,
And the far-off Friulan snow;
The land and sea, the sun and shade,
And the blue even lamp-inlaid.

For this, for these, for all, O friend,
For your whole book from end to end –
For Paron Piero's mutton-ham –
I your defaulting debtor am.

Perchance, reviving, yet may I
30 To your sea-paven city hie,
And in a *felze*, some day yet
Light at your pipe my cigarette.

XV Et Tu in Arcadia Vixisti

To R. A. M. S.

In ancient tales, O friend, thy spirit dwelt;
There, from of old, thy childhood passed; and there
High expectation, high delights and deeds,
Thy fluttering heart with hope and terror moved.
And thou hast heard of yore the Blatant Beast,

And Roland's horn, and that war-scattering shout
Of all-unarmed Achilles, ægis-crowned.
And perilous lands thou sawest, sounding shores
And seas and forests drear, island and dale
10   And mountain dark. For thou with Tristram rod'st
Or Bedevere, in farthest Lyonesse.
Thou hadst a booth in Samarcand, whereat
Side-looking Magians trafficked; thence, by night,
An Afreet snatched thee, and with wings upbore
Beyond the Aral mount; or, hoping gain,
Thou, with a jar of money, didst embark,
For Balsorah, by sea. But chiefly thou
In that clear air took'st life; in Arcady
The haunted, land of song; and by the wells
20   Where most the gods frequent. There Chiron old,
In the Pelethronian antre, taught thee lore:
The plants, he taught, and by the shining stars
In forests dim to steer. There hast thou seen
Immortal Pan dance secret in a glade,
And, dancing, roll his eyes; these, where they fell,
Shed glee, and through the congregated oaks
A flying horror winged; while all the earth
To the god's pregnant footing thrilled within.
Or whiles, beside the sobbing stream, he breathed,
30   In his clutched pipe, unformed and wizard strains.
Divine yet brutal; which the forest heard,
And thou, with awe; and far upon the plain
The unthinking ploughman started and gave ear.

Now things there are that, upon him who sees,
A strong vocation lay; and strains there are
That whoso hears shall hear for evermore.
For evermore thou hear'st immortal Pan
And those melodious godheads, ever young
And ever quiring, on the mountains old.

40   What was this earth, child of the gods, to thee?
Forth from thy dreamland thou, a dreamer, cam'st,
And in thine ears the olden music rang,

And in thy mind the doings of the dead,
And those heroic ages long forgot.
To a so fallen earth, alas! too late,
Alas! in evil days, thy steps return,
To list at noon for nightingales, to grow
A dweller on the beach till Argo come
That came long since, a lingerer by the pool
50   Where that desirèd angel bathes no more.

As when the Indian to Dakota comes,
Or farthest Idaho, and where he dwelt,
He with his clan, a humming city finds;
Thereon awhile, amazed, he stares, and then
To right and leftward, like a questing dog,
Seeks first the ancestral altars, then the hearth
Long cold with rains, and where old terror lodged,
And where the dead. So thee undying Hope,
With all her pack, hunts screaming through the years:
60   Here, there, thou fleëst; but nor here nor there
The pleasant gods abide, the glory dwells.

That, that was not Apollo, not the god.
This was not Venus, though she Venus seemed
A moment. And though fair yon river move,
She, all the way, from disenchanted fount
To seas unhallowed runs; the gods forsook
Long since her trembling rushes; from her plains
Disconsolate, long since adventure fled;
And now although the inviting river flows,
70   And every poplared cape, and every bend
Or willowy islet, win upon thy soul
And to thy hopeful shallop whisper speed;
Yet hope not thou at all; hope is no more;
And O, long since the golden groves are dead,
The faery cities vanished from the land!

XVI   To W. E. Henley

The year runs through her phases; rain and sun,
Springtime and summer pass; winter succeeds;
But one pale season rules the house of death.
Cold falls the imprisoned daylight; fell disease
By each lean pallet squats, and pain and sleep
Toss gaping on the pillows.

                                        But O thou!
Uprise and take thy pipe. Bid music flow,
Strains by good thoughts attended, like the spring
The swallows follow over land and sea.
10   Pain sleeps at once; at once, with open eyes,
Dozing despair awakes. The shepherd sees
His flock come bleating home; the seaman hears
Once more the cordage rattle. Airs of home!
Youth, love and roses blossom; the gaunt ward
Dislimns and disappears, and, opening out,
Show brooks and forests, and the blue beyond
Of mountains.

                                Small the pipe; but O! do thou,
Peak-faced and suffering piper, blow therein
The dirge of heroes dead; and to these sick,
20   These dying, sound the triumph over death.
Behold! each greatly breathes; each tastes a joy
Unknown before, in dying; for each knows
A hero dies with him – though unfulfilled,
Yet conquering truly – and not dies in vain.

So is pain cheered, death comforted; the house
Of sorrow smiles to listen. Once again –
O thou, Orpheus and Heracles, the bard
And the deliverer, touch the stops again!

XVIII The Mirror Speaks

Where the bells peal far at sea
Cunning fingers fashioned me.
There on palace walls I hung
While that Consuelo sung;
But I heard, though I listened well,
Never a note, never a trill,
Never a beat of the chiming bell.
There I hung and looked, and there
In my gray face, faces fair
10 Shone from under shining hair.

Well I saw the poising head,
But the lips moved and nothing said;
And when lights were in the hall,
Silent moved the dancers all.

So awhile I glowed, and then
Fell on dusty days and men;
Long I slumbered packed in straw,
Long I none but dealers saw;
Till before my silent eye
20 One that sees came passing by.

Now with an outlandish grace,
To the sparkling fire I face
In the blue room at Skerryvore;
Where I wait until the door
Open, and the Prince of Men,
Henry James, shall come again.

XXI Requiem

Under the wide and starry sky,
Dig the grave and let me lie.
Glad did I live and gladly die,
   And I laid me down with a will.

This be the verse you grave for me:
Here he lies where he longed to be;
Home is the sailor, home from sea,
   And the hunter home from the hill.

XXVI The Sick Child

Child.
O mother, lay your hand on my brow!
O mother, mother, where am I now?
Why is the room so gaunt and great?
Why am I lying awake so late?

Mother.
Fear not at all: the night is still.
Nothing is here that means you ill –
Nothing but lamps the whole town through,
And never a child awake but you.

Child.
Mother, mother, speak low in my ear,
Some of the things are so great and near,
Some are so small and far away,
I have a fear that I cannot say.
What have I done, and what do I fear,
And why are you crying, mother dear?

Mother.
Out in the city, sounds begin.
Thank the kind God, the carts come in!
An hour or two more, and God is so kind,
The day shall be blue in the window-blind,
Then shall my child go sweetly asleep,
20   And dream of the birds and the hills of sheep.

XXX *A Portrait*

I am a kind of farthing dip,
   Unfriendly to the nose and eyes;
A blue-behinded ape, I skip
   Upon the trees of Paradise.

At mankind's feast, I take my place
   In solemn, sanctimonious state,
And have the air of saying grace
   While I defile the dinner plate.

I am 'the smiler with the knife,'
10   The battener upon garbage, I –
Dear Heaven, with such a rancid life,
   Were it not better far to die?

Yet still, about the human pale,
   I love to scamper, love to race,
To swing by my irreverent tail
   All over the most holy place;

And when at length, some golden day,
   The unfailing sportsman, aiming at,
Shall bag, me – all the world shall say:
20   *Thank God, and there's an end of that!*

XXXV Skerryvore: The Parallel

Here all is sunny, and when the truant gull
Skims the green level of the lawn, his wing
Dispetals roses; here the house is framed
Of kneaded brick and the plumed mountain pine,
Such clay as artists fashion and such wood
As the tree-climbing urchin breaks. But there
Eternal granite hewn from the living isle
And dowelled with brute iron, rears a tower
That from its wet foundation to its crown
10 Of glittering glass, stands, in the sweep of winds,
Immovable, immortal, eminent.

XXXVIII 'My body which my dungeon is'

My body which my dungeon is,
And yet my parks and palaces:
    Which is so great that there I go
All the day long to and fro,
And when the night begins to fall
Throw down my bed and sleep, while all
The building hums and wakefulness –
Even as a child of savages
When evening takes her on her way,
10 (She having roamed a summer's day
Along the mountain-sides and scalp)
Sleeps in an antre of that alp:
    Which is so broad and high that there,
As in the topless fields of air,
My fancy soars like to a kite
And faints in the blue infinite:
    Which is so strong, my strongest throes
And the rough world's besieging blows
Not break it, and so weak withal,
20 Death ebbs and flows in its loose wall

As the green sea in fishers' nets,
And tops its topmost parapets:
 Which is so wholly mine that I
Can wield its whole artillery,
And mine so little, that my soul
Dwells in perpetual control,
And I but think and speak and do
As my dead fathers move me to:
 If this born body of my bones
30 The beggared soul so barely owns,
What money passsed from hand to hand,
What creeping custom of the land,
What deed of author or assign,
Can make a house a thing of mine?

BOOK TWO – IN SCOTS*

I The Maker to Posterity

Far 'yont amang the years to be
When a' we think, an' a' we see,
An' a' we luve, 's been dung ajee
  By time's rouch shouther,
An' what was richt and wrang for me
  Lies mangled throu'ther,

It's possible – it's hardly mair –
That some ane, ripin' after lear –
Some auld professor or young heir,
10 If still there's either –
May find an' read me, an' be sair
  Perplexed, puir brither!

---

*. See Appendix for RLS's Note on Scots Language, from *Underwoods*.

'*What tongue does your auld bookie speak?*'
He'll spier; an' I, his mou to steik:
'*No bein' fit to write in Greek,*
  I wrote in Lallan,
Dear to my heart as the peat reek,
  Auld as Tantallon.

'*Few spak it than, an' noo there's nane.*
20 *My puir auld sangs lie a' their lane,*
Their sense, that aince was braw an plain,
  Tint a'thegether,
Like runes upon a standin' stane
  Amang the heather.

'*But think not you the brae to speel;*
You, tae, maun chow the bitter peel;
For a' your lear, for a' your skeel,
  Ye're nane sae lucky;
An' things are mebbe waur than weel
30 *For you, my buckie.*

'*The hale concern (baith hens an' eggs,*
Baith books an' writers, stars an' clegs)
Noo stachers upon lowsent legs
  An' wears awa';
The tack o' mankind, near the dregs,
  Rins unco' law.

'*Your book, that in some braw new tongue,*
Ye wrote or prentit, preached or sung,
Will still be just a bairn, an' young
40 *In fame an' years,*
Whan the hale planet's guts are dung
  About your ears;

'An' you, sair gruppin' to a spar
Or whammled wi' some bleezin' star,
Cryin' to ken whaur deil ye are,
        Hame, France, or Flanders –
Whang sindry like a railway car
        An' flie in danders.'

II Ille Terrarum

Frae nirly, nippin', Eas'lan' breeze,
Frae Norlan' snaw, an' haar o' seas,
Weel happit in your gairden trees,
        A bonny bit,
Atween the muckle Pentland's knees,
        Secure ye sit.

Beeches an' aiks entwine their theek,
An' firs, a stench, auld-farrant clique.
A' simmer day, your chimleys reek,
10   Couthy and bien;
An' here an' there your windies keek
        Amang the green.

A pickle plats an' paths an' posies,
A wheen auld gillyflowers an' roses:
A ring o' wa's the hale encloses
        Frae sheep or men;
An' there the auld housie beeks an' dozes,
        A' by her lane.

The gairdner crooks his weary back
20   A' day in the pitaty-track,
Or mebbe stops awhile to crack
        Wi' Jane the cook,
Or at some buss, worm-eaten-black,
        To gie a look.

Frae the high hills the curlew ca's;
The sheep gang baaing by the wa's;
Or whiles a clan o' roosty craws
  Cangle thegether;
The wild bees seek the gairden raws,
30   Weariet wi' heather.

Or in the gloamin' douce an' gray
The sweet-throat mavis tunes her lay;
The herd comes linkin' doun the brae;
  An' by degrees
The muckle silver müne maks way
  Amang the trees.

Here aft hae I, wi' sober heart,
For meditation sat apairt,
When orra loves or kittle art
40   Perplexed my mind;
Here socht a balm for ilka smart
  O' humankind.

Here aft, weel neukit by my lane,
Wi' Horace, or perhaps Montaigne,
The mornin' hours hae come an' gane
  Abüne my held –
I wadnae gi'en a chucky-stane
  For a' I'd read.

But noo the auld city, street by street,
50 An' winter fu' o' snaw an' sleet,
Awhile shut in my gangrel feet
  An' goavin' mettle;
Noo is the soopit ingle sweet,
  An' liltin' kettle.

An' noo the winter winds complain;
Cauld lies the glaur in ilka lane;
On draigled hizzie, tautit wean
      An' drucken lads,
In the mirk nicht, the winter rain
60   Dribbles an' blads.

Whan bugles frae the Castle rock,
An' beaten drums wi' dowie shock,
Wauken, at cauld-rife sax o'clock,
      My chitterin' frame,
I mind me on the kintry cock,
      The kintry hame.

I mind me on yon bonny bield;
An' Fancy traivels far afield
To gaither a' that gairdens yield
70   O' sun an' Simmer:
To hearten up a dowie chield,
      Fancy's the limmer!

III 'When aince Aprile has fairly come'

When aince Aprile has fairly come,
An' birds may bigg in winter's lum,
An' pleisure's spreid for a' and some
      O' whatna state,
Love, wi' her auld recruitin' drum,
      Than taks the gate.

The heart plays dunt wi' main an' micht;
The lasses' een are a' sae bricht,
Their dresses are sae braw an' ticht,
10   The bonny birdies! —
Puir winter virtue at the sicht
      Gangs heels ower hurdies.

An' aye as love frae land to land
Tirls the drum wi' eident hand,
A' men collect at her command,
  Toun-bred or land'art,
An' follow in a denty band
  Her gaucy standart.

An' I, wha sang o' rain an' snaw,
20 An' weary winter weel awa',
Noo busk me in a jacket braw,
  An' tak my place
I' the ram-stam, harum-scarum raw,
  Wi' smilin' face.

IV   A Mile an' a Bittock

A mile an' a bittock, a mile or twa,
Abüne, the burn, ayont the law,
Davie an' Donal' an' Cherlie an' a',
  An' the müne was shinin' clearly!

Ane went hame wi' the ither, an' then
The ither went hame wi' the ither twa men,
An' baith wad return him the service again,
  An' the müne was shinin' clearly!

The clocks were chappin' in house an' ha',
10 Eleeven, twal an' ane an' twa;
An' the guidman's face was turnt to the wa',
  An' the müne was shinin' clearly!

A wind got up frae affa the sea,
It blew the stars as clear's could be,
It blew in the een of a' o' the three,
  An' the müne was shinin' clearly!

Noo, Davie was first to get sleep in his head,
'The best o' frien's maun twine,' he said;
'I'm weariet, an' here I'm awa' to my bed.'
20   An' the müne was shinin' clearly!

Twa o' them walkin' an' crackin' their lane,
The mornin' licht cam gray an' plain,
An' the birds they yammert on stick an' stane,
     An' the müne was shinin' clearly!

O years ayont, O years awa',
My lads, ye'll mind whate'er befa' –
My lads, ye'll mind on the beild o' the law,
     When the müne was shinin' clearly.

V A Lowden Sabbath Morn

The clinkum-clank o' Sabbath bells
Noo to the hoastin' rookery swells,
Noo faintin' laigh in shady dells,
     Sounds far an' near,
An' through the simmer kintry tells
     Its tale o' cheer.

An' noo, to that melodious play,
A' deidly awn the quiet sway –
A' ken their solemn holiday,
10   Bestial an' human,
The singin' lintie on the brae,
     The restin' plou'man.

He, mair than a' the lave o' men,
His week completit joys to ken;
Half-dressed, he daunders out an' in,
     Perplext wi' leisure;
An' his raxt limbs he'll rax again
     Wi' painfü' pleesure.

The steerin' mither strange afit
20 Noo shoos the bairnies but a bit;
Noo cries them ben, their Sinday shüit
        To scart upon them,
Or sweeties in their pouch to pit,
        Wi' blessin's on them.

The lasses, clean frae tap to taes,
Are busked in crunklin' underclaes;
The gartened hose, the weel-filled stays,
        The nakit shift,
A' bleached on bonny greens for days,
30   An' white's the drift.

An' noo to face the kirkward mile:
The guidman's hat o' dacent style,
The blackit shoon, we noo maun fyle
        As white's the miller:
A waefü' peety tae, to spile
        The warth o' siller.

Our Marg'et, aye sae keen to crack,
Douce-stappin' in the stoury track,
Her emeralt goun a' kiltit back
40   Frae snawy coats,
White-ankled, leads the kirkward pack
        Wi' Dauvit Groats.

A thocht ahint, in runkled breeks,
A' spiled wi' lyin' by for weeks,
The guidman follows closs, an' cleiks
        The sonsie missis;
His sarious face at aince bespeaks
        The day that this is.

And aye an' while we nearer draw
50   To whaur the kirkton lies alaw,
Mair neebours, comin' saft an' slaw
        Frae here an' there,
The thicker thrang the gate an' caw
        The stour in air.

But hark! the bells frae nearer clang;
To rowst the slaw, their sides they bang;
An' see! black coats a'ready thrang
        The green kirkyaird;
And at the yett, the chestnuts spang
60   That brocht the laird.

The solemn elders at the plate
Stand drinkin' deep the pride o' state:
The practised hands as gash an' great
        As Lords o' Session;
The later named, a wee thing blate
        In their expression.

The prentit stanes that mark the deid,
Wi' lengthened lip, the sarious read;
Syne wag a moraleesin' heid,
70   An' then an' there
Their hirplin' practice an' their creed
        Try hard to square.

It's here our Merren lang has lain,
A wee bewast the table-stane;
An' yon's the grave o' Sandy Blane;
        An' further ower,
The mither's brithers, dacent men!
        Lie a' the fower.

Here the guidman sall bide awee
80   To dwall amang the deid; to see
Auld faces clear in fancy's e'e;
            Belike to hear
Auld voices fa'in saft an' slee
            On fancy's ear.

Thus, on the day o' solemn things,
The bell that in the steeple swings
To fauld a scaittered faim'ly rings
            Its walcome screed;
An' just a wee thing nearer brings
90   The quick an' deid.

But noo the bell is ringin' in;
To tak their places, folk begin;
The minister himsel' will shüne
            Be up the gate,
Filled fu' wi' clavers about sin
            An' man's estate.

The tünes are up – *French*, to be shüre,
The faithfü' *French*, an' twa-three mair;
The auld prezentor, hoastin' sair,
100   Wales out the portions,
An' yirks the tüne into the air
            Wi' queer contortions.

Follows the prayer, the readin' next,
An' than the fisslin' for the text –
The twa-three last to find it, vext
            But kind o' proud;
An' than the peppermints are raxed,
            An' southernwood.

For noo's the time whan pows are seen
110   Nid noddin' like a mandareen;
When tenty mithers stap a preen
            In sleepin' weans;
An' nearly half the parochine
            Forget their pains.

There's just a waukrif' twa or three:
Thrawn commentautors sweet to 'gree,
Weans glowrin' at the bumlin' bee
            On windie-glasses,
Or lads that tak a keek a-glee
120   At sonsie lasses.

Himsel', meanwhile, frae whaur he cocks
An' bobs belaw the soundin'-box,
The treesures of his words unlocks
            Wi' prodigality,
An' deals some unco dingin' knocks
            To infidality.

Wi' sappy unction, hoo he burkes
The hopes o' men that trust in works,
Expounds the fau'ts o' ither kirks,
130   An' shaws the best o' them
No muckle better than mere Turks,
            When a's confessed o' them.

Bethankit! what a bonny creed!
What mair would ony Christian need? –
The braw words rumm'le ower his heid,
            Nor steer the sleeper;
And in their restin' graves, the deid
            Sleep aye the deeper.

VI The Spaewife

O, I wad like to ken – to the beggar-wife says I –
Why chops are guid to brander and nane sae guid to fry.
An' siller, that's sae braw to keep, is brawer still to gi'e.
– *It's gey an' easy spierin'*, says the beggar-wife to me.

O, I wad like to ken – to the beggar-wife says I –
Hoo a' things come to be whaur we find them when we try,
The lasses in their claes an' the fishes in the sea.
– *It's gey an' easy spierin'*, says the beggar-wife to me.

O, I wad like to ken – to the beggar-wife says I –
10   Why lads are a' to sell an' lasses a' to buy;
An' naebody for dacency but barely twa or three.
– *It's gey an' easy spierin'*, says the beggar-wife to me.

O, I wad like to ken – to the beggar-wife says I –
Gin death's as shüre to men as killin' is to kye,
Why God has filled the yearth sae fu' o' tasty things to pree.
– *It's gey an' easy spierin'*, says the beggar-wife to me.

O, I wad like to ken – to the beggar wife says I –
The reason o' the cause an' the wherefore o' the why,
Wi' mony anither riddle brings the tears into my e'e.
20   – *It's gey an' easy spierin'*, says the beggar-wife to me.

VII The Blast – *1875*

It's rainin'. Weet's the gairden sod,
Weet the lang roads whaur gangrels plod
A maist unceevil thing o' God
            In mid July –
If ye'll just curse the sneckdraw, dod!
            An' sae wull I!

He's a braw place in Heev'n, ye ken,
An' lea's us puir, forjaskit men
Clamjamfried in the but and ben
          He ca's the earth –
A wee bit inconvenient den
          No muckle worth;

An' whiles, at orra times, keeks out,
Sees what puir mankind are about;
An' if He can, I've little doubt,
          Upsets their plans;
He hates a' mankind, brainch and root,
          An' a' that's man's.

An' whiles, whan they tak heart again,
An' life i' the sun looks braw an' plain,
Doun comes a jaw o' droukin' rain
          Upon their honours –
God sends a spate outower the plain,
          Or mebbe thun'ers.

Lord safe us, life's an unco thing!
Simmer an' Winter, Yule an' Spring,
The damned, dour-heartit seasons bring
          A feck o' trouble.
I wadnae try't to be a king –
          No, nor for double.

But since we're in it, willy-nilly,
We maun be watchfü,' wise an' skilly,
An' no mind ony ither billy,
          Lassie nor God.
But drink – that's my best counsel till 'e:
          Sae tak the nod.

VIII   *The Counterblast – 1886*

My bonny man, the warld, it's true,
Was made for neither me nor you;
It's just a place to warstle through,
    As Job confessed o't;
And aye the best that we'll can do
    Is mak the best o't.

There's rowth o' wrang, I'm free to say;
The simmer brunt, the winter blae,
The face of earth a' fyled wi' clay
10   An' dour wi' chuckies,
An' life a rough an' land'art play
    For country buckies.

An' food's anither name for clart;
An' beasts an' brambles bite an' scart;
An' what would WE be like, my heart!
    If bared o' claethin'?
– Aweel, I cannae mend your cart:
    It's that or naethin'.

A feck o' folk frae first to last
20 Have through this queer experience passed;
Twa-three, I ken, just damn an' blast
    The hale transaction;
But twa-three ithers, east an' wast,
    Fand satisfaction.

Whaur braid the briery muirs expand,
A waefü' an' a weary land,
The bumblebees, a gowden band,
    Are blithely hingin';
An' there the canty wanderer fand
30   The laverock singin'.

Trout in the burn grow great as herr'n';
The simple sheep can find their fair'n;
The wind blaws clean about the cairn
          Wi' caller air;
The muircock an' the barefit bairn
          Are happy there.

Sic-like the howes o' life to some:
Green loans whaur they ne'er fash their thumb,
But mark the muckle winds that come,
40   Soopin' an' cool,
Or hear the powrin' burnie drum
          In the shilfa's pool.

The evil wi' the guid they tak;
They ca' a gray thing gray, no black;
To a steigh brae, a stubborn back
          Addressin' daily;
An' up the rude, unbieldy track
          O' life, gang gaily.

What you would like's a palace ha',
50   Or Sinday parlour dink an' braw
Wi' a' things ordered in a raw
          By denty leddies.
Weel, then, ye cannae hae't: that's a'
          That to be said is.

An' since at life ye've taen the grue,
An' winnae blithely hirsle through,
Ye've fund the very thing to do –
          That's to drink speerit;
An' shüne we'll hear the last o' you –
          An' blithe to hear it!

The shoon ye coft, the life ye lead,
Ithers will heir when aince ye're deid;
They'll heir your tasteless bite o' breid,
    An' find it sappy;
They'll to your dulefu' house succeed,
    An' there be happy.

As whan a glum an' fractious wean
Has sat an' sullened by his lane
Till, wi' a rowstin' skelp, he's taen
70   An' shoo'd to bed –
The ither bairns a' fa' to play'n',
    As gleg's a gled.

IX *The Counterblast Ironical*

It's strange that God should fash to frame
    The yearth and lift sae hie,
An' clean forget to explain the same
    To a gentleman like me.

They gutsy, donnered ither folk,
    Their weird they weel may dree,
But why present a pig in a poke
    To a gentleman like me?

They ither folk their parritch eat
10   An' sup their sugared tea;
But the mind is no to be wyled wi' meat
    Wi' a gentleman like me.

They ither folk, they court their joes
    At gloamin' on the lea;
But they're made of a commoner clay, I suppose,
    Than a gentleman like me.

They ither folk, for richt or wrang,
    They suffer, bleed, or dee;
But a' thir things are an emp'y sang
20   To a gentleman like me.

It's a different thing that I demand,
    Tho' humble as can be –
A statement fair in my Maker's hand
    To a gentleman like me:

A clear account writ fair an' broad,
    An' a plain apologie;
Or the deevil a ceevil word to God
    From a gentleman like me.

X *Their Laureate to an Academy Class Dinner Club*

Dear Thamson class, whaure'er I gang
It aye comes ower me wi' a spang:
    'Lordsake! they Thamson lads – (deil hang
        Or else Lord mend them!) –
An' that wanchancy annual sang
        I ne'er can send them!'

Straucht, at the name, a trusty tyke,
My conscience girrs ahint the dyke;
Straucht on my hinderlands I fyke
10   To find a rhyme t' ye;
Pleased – although mebbe no pleased-like –
    To gie my time t'ye.

'Weel,' an' says you, wi' heavin' breist,
'Sae far, sae guid, but what's the neist?
Yearly we gaither to the feast,
    A' hopefü' men –
Yearly we skelloch "Hang the beast –
    Nae sang again!"'

My lads, an' what am I to say?
20 Ye shüurely ken the Muse's way:
Yestreen, as gleg's a tyke – the day,
    Thrawn like a cuddy:
Her conduc', that to her's a play,
    Deith to a body.

Aft whan I sat an' made my mane,
Aft whan I laboured burd-alane
Fishin' for rhymes an' finding' nane,
    Or nane were fit for ye –
Ye judged me cauld's a chucky stane –
30   No car'n' a bit for ye!

But saw ye ne'er some pingein' bairn
As weak as a pitaty-par'n' –
Less üsed wi' guidin' horse-shoe airn
    Than steerin' crowdie –
Packed aff his lane, by moss an' cairn,
    To ca' the howdie.

Wae's me, for the puir callant than!
He wambles like a poke o' bran,
An' the lowse rein, as hard's he can,
40   Pu's, trem'lin' handit;
Till, blaff! upon his hinderlan'
    Behauld him landit.

Sick-like – I awn the weary fac' –
Whan on my Muse the gate I tak,
An' see her gleed e'e raxin' back
    To keek ahint her; –
To me, the brig o' Heev'n gangs black
    As blackest winter.

'Lordsake! we're aff,' thinks I, *'but whaur?*
50   *On what abhorred an' whinny scaur,*
Or whammled in what sea o' glaur,
          Will she desert me?
An' will she just disgrace? or waur –
          Will she no hurt me?'

Kittle the quaere! But at least
The day I've backed the fashious beast,
While she, wi' mony a spang an' reist,
          Flang heels ower bonnet;
An' a' triumphant – for your feast,
60   Hae! there's your sonnet!

XI *Embro Hie Kirk*

The Lord Himsel' in former days
Waled out the proper tünes for praise
An' named the proper kind o' claes
          For folk to preach in:
Preceese and in the chief o' ways
          Important teachin'.

He ordered a' things late and air';
He ordered folk to stand at prayer.
(Although I cannae just mind where
10   He gave the warnin'.)
An' pit pomatum on their hair
          On Sabbath mornin'.

The hale o' life by His commands
Was ordered to a body's hands;
But see! this *corpus juris* stands
          By a' forgotten;
An' God's religion in a' lands
          Is deid an' rotten.

While thus the lave o' mankind's lost,
O' Scotland still God maks His boast –
Puir Scotland, on whase barren coast
      A score or twa
Auld wives wi' mutches an' a hoast
      Still keep His law.

In Scotland, a wheen canty, plain,
Douce, kintry-leevin' folk retain
The Truth – or did so aince – alane
      Of a' men leevin';
An' noo just twa o' them remain –
      Just Begg an' Niven.

For noo, unfaithfü', to the Lord
Auld Scotland joins the rebel horde;
Her human hymn-books on the board
      She noo displays:
An' Embro Hie Kirk's been restored
      In popish ways.

O *punctum temporis* for action
To a' o' the reformin' faction,
If yet, by ony act or paction,
      Thocht, word, or sermon,
This dark an' damnable transaction
      Micht yet determine!

For see – as Doctor Begg explains –
Hoo easy 't's düne! a pickle weans,
Wha in the Hie Street gaither stanes
      By his instruction,
The uncovenantit, pentit panes
      Ding to destruction.

Up, Niven, or ower late – an' dash
50 Laigh in the glaur that carnal hash;
Let spires and pews wi' gran' stramash
        Thegether fa';
The rumlin' kist o' whustles smash
        In pieces sma'.

Noo choose ye out a walie hammer;
About the knottit buttress clam'er;
Alang the steep roof stoyt an' stammer,
        A gate mis-chancy;
On the aul' spire, the bells' hie cha'mer,
60   Dance your bit dancie.

Ding, devel, dunt, destroy, an' ruin,
Wi' carnal stanes the square bestrewin',
Till your loud chaps frae Kyle to Fruin,
        Frae Hell to Heeven,
Tell the guid wark that baith are doin' –
        Baith Begg an' Niven.

XII The Scotsman's Return from Abroad

In a letter from Mr Thomson to Mr Johnstone

In mony a foreign pairt I've been,
An' money an unco ferlie seen,
Since, Mr Johnstone, you and I
Last walkit upon Cocklerye.
Wi' gleg, observant een, I pass't
By sea an' land, through East an' Wast,
And still in ilka age an' station
Saw naething but abomination.
In thir uncovenantit lands
10 The gangrel Scot uplifts his hands
At lack of a' sectarian füsh'n,
An' cauld religious destitūtion.

He rins, puir man, frae place to place,
Tries a' their graceless means o' grace,
Preacher on preacher, kirk on kirk –
This yin a stot an' thon a stirk –
A bletherin' clan, no warth a preen,
As bad as Smith of Aiberdeen!

At last, across the weary faem,
20   Frae far, outlandish pairts I came.
On ilka side o' me I fand
Fresh tokens o' my native land.
Wi' whatna joy I hailed them a' –
The hilltaps standin' raw by raw,
The public house, the Hielan' birks,
And a' the bonny U.P. kirks!
But maistly thee, the bluid o' Scots,
Frae Maidenkirk to John o' Grots,
The king o' drinks, as I conceive it,
30   Talisker, Isla, or Glenlivet!

For after years wi' a pockmantie
Frae Zanzibar to Alicante,
In mony a fash and sair affliction
I gie't as my sincere conviction –
Of a' their foreign tricks an' pliskies,
I maist abominate their whiskies.
Nae doot, themsel's, they ken it weel,
An' wi' a hash o' leemon peel,
And ice an' siccan filth, they ettle
40   The stawsome kind o' goo to settle;
Sic wersh apothecary's broos wi'
As Scotsmen scorn to fyle their moo's wi'.

An' man, I was a blithe hame–comer
Whan first I syndit out my rummer.
Ye should hae seen me then, wi' care
The less important pairts prepare;
Syne, weel contentit wi' it a',
Pour in the speerits wi' a jaw!

I didnae drink, I didnae speak –
50   I only snowkit up the reek.
I was sae pleased therein to paidle,
I sat an' plowtered wi' my ladle.

An' blithe was I, the morrow's morn,
To daunder through the stookit corn,
And after a' my strange mishanters,
Sit doun amang my ain dissenters.
An', man, it was a joy to me
The pu'pit an' the pews to see,
The pennies dirlin' in the plate,
60   The elders lookin' on in state;
An' 'mang the first, as it befell,
Wha should I see, sir, but yoursel'.

I was, and I will no deny it,
At the first gliff a hantle tryit.
To see yoursel' in sic a station –
It seemed a doubtfü' dispensation.
The feelin' was a mere digression;
For shüne I understood the session,
An' mindin' Aiken an' M'Neil,
70   I wondered they had düne sae weel.
I saw I had mysel' to blame;
For had I but remained at hame,
Aiblins – though no ava' deservin' 't –
They micht hae named your humble servant.

The kirk was filled, the door was steeked;
Up to the pu'pit ance I keeked;
I was mair pleased than I can tell –
It was the minister himsel'!
Proud, proud was I to see his face,
80   After sae lang awa' frae grace.
Pleased as I was, I'm no denyin'
Some maitters were not edifyin';
For first I fand – an' here was news! –
Mere hymn-books cockin' in the pews –

A humanised abomination,
Unfit for ony congregation.
Syne, while I still was on the tenter,
I scunnered at the new prezentor;
I thocht him gesterin' an' cauld –
90   A sair declension frae the auld.

Syne, as though a' the faith was wreckit,
The prayer was not what I'd exspeckit.
Himsel', as it appeared to me,
Was no the man he üsed to be.
But just as I was growin' vext
He waled a maist judeecious text,
An', launchin' into his prelections,
Swoopt, wi' a skirl, on a' defections.

O what a gale was on my speerit
100   To hear the p'ints o' doctrine clearit,
And a' the horrors o' damnation
Set furth wi' faithfü' ministration!
Nae shauchlin' testimony here –
We were a' damned, an' that was clear.
I owned, wi' gratitude an' wonder,
He was a pleisure to sit under.

XIII 'Late in the nicht in bed I lay'

Late in the nicht in bed I lay,
The winds were at their weary play,
An' tirlin' wa's an' skirlin' wae
      Through Heev'n they battered;
On-ding o' hail, on-blaff o' spray,
      The tempest blattered.

The masoned house it dinled through;
It dung the ship, it cowped the coo';
The rankit aiks it overthrew,

10   Had braved a' weathers;
The strang sea-gleds it took an' blew
          Awa' like feathers.

The thrawes o' fear on a' were shed,
An' the hair rose, an' slumber fled,
An' lichts were lit an' prayers were said
          Through a' the kintry;
An' the cauld terror clum in bed
          Wi' a' an' sindry.

To hear in the pit-mirk on hie
20   The brangled collieshangie flie,
The warl', they thocht, wi' land an' sea,
          Itsel' wad cowpit;
An' for auld airn, the smashed debris
          By God be rowpit.

Meanwhile frae far Aldeboran
To folks wi' talescopes in han',
O' ships that cowpit, winds that ran,
          Nae sign was seen,
But the wee warl' in sunshine span
30   As bricht's a preen.

I, tae, by God's especial grace,
Dwall denty in a bieldy place,
Wi' hosened feet, wi' shaven face,
          Wi' dacent mainners:
A grand example to the race
          O' tautit sinners!

The wind may blaw, the heathen rage,
The deil may start on the rampage;
The sick in bed, the thief in cage –
40   What's a' to me?
Cosh in my house, a sober sage,
          I sit an' see.

An' whiles the bluid spangs to my bree,
To lie sae saft, to live sae free,
While better men maun do an' die
    In unco places.
'*Whaur's God?*' I cry, an' '*Whae is me*
    To hae sic graces?'

I mind the fecht the sailors keep,
But fire or can'le, rest or sleep,
In darkness an' the muckle deep;
    An' mind beside
The herd that on the hills o' sheep
    Has wandered wide.

I mind me on the hoastin' weans —
The penny joes on causey stanes —
The auld folk wi' the crazy banes,
    Baith auld an' puir,
That aye maun thole the winds an' rains
    An' labour sair.

An' whiles I'm kind o' pleased a blink
An' kind o' fleyed forby, to think,
For a' my rowth o' meat an' drink
    An' waste o' crumb,
I'll mebbe have to thole wi' skink
    In Kingdom Come.

For God whan jowes the Judgment bell,
Wi' His ain Hand, His Leevin' Sel',
Sall ryve the guid (as Prophets tell)
    Frae them that had it;
And in the reamin' pat o' Hell,
    The rich be scaddit.

O Lord, if this indeed be sae,
Let daw that sair an' happy day!
Again' the warl', grawn auld an' gray,
        Up wi' your aixe!
An' let the puir enjoy their play –
        I'll thole my paiks.

XIV My Conscience!

Of a' the ills that flesh can fear,
The loss o' frien's, the lack o' gear,
A yowlin' tyke, a glandered mear,
        A lassie's nonsense –
There's just ae thing I cannae bear,
        An' that's my conscience.

Whan day (an' a' excūse) has gane,
An' wark is dūne, and duty's plain,
An' to my chalmer a' my lane
10   I creep apairt,
My conscience! hoo the yammerin' pain
        Stends to my heart!

A' day wi' various ends in view
The hairsts o' time I had to pu',
An' made a hash wad staw a soo,
        Let me be a man! –
My conscience! whan my han's were fu',
        Whaur were ye than?

An' there were a' the lures o' life,
20 There pleesure skirlin' on the fife,
There anger, wi' the hotchin' knife
        Ground shairp in Hell –
My conscience! – you that's like a wife! –
        Whaur was yoursel'?

I ken it fine: just waitin' here,
To gar the evil waur appear,
To clart the guid, confūse the clear,
      Mis-ca' the great,
My conscience! an' to raise a steer
30   Whan a's ower late.

Sic-like, some tyke grawn auld and blind,
Whan thieves brok' through the gear to p'ind,
Has lain his dozened length an' grinned
      At the disaster;
An' the morn's mornin', wud's the wind,
      Yokes on his master.

XV *To Doctor John Brown*

(Whan the dear doctor, dear to a',
Was still among us here belaw,
I set my pipes his praise to blaw
*   Wi' a' my speerit;*
But noo, Dear Doctor! he's awa',
*   An' ne'er can hear it.)*

By Lyne and Tyne, by Thames and Tees,
By a' the various river-Dee's,
In Mars and Manors 'yont the seas
     Or here at hame,
Whaure'er there's kindly folk to please,
     They ken your name.

They ken your name, they ken your tyke
They ken the honey from your byke;
But mebbe after a' your fyke,
10   (The trüth to tell)
It's just your honest Rab they like,
     An' no yoursel'.

As at the gowff, some canny play'r
Should tee a common ba' wi' care –
Should flourish and deeleever fair
      His souple shintie –
An' the ba' rise into the air,
      A leevin' lintie:

Sae in the game we writers play,
20 There comes to some a bonny day,
When a dear ferlie shall repay
      Their years o' strife,
An' like your Rab, their things o' clay,
      Spreid wings o' life.

Ye scarce deserved it, I'm afraid –
You that had never learned the trade,
But just some idle mornin' strayed
      Into the schüle,
An' picked the fiddle up an' played
30   Like Neil himsel'.

Your e'e was gleg, your fingers dink;
Ye didnae fash yoursel' to think,
But wove, as fast as puss can link,
      Your denty wab:
Ye stapped your pen into the ink,
      An' there was Rab!

Sinsyne, whaure'er your fortune lay
By dowie den, by canty brae,
Simmer an' winter, nicht an' day,
40   Rab was aye wi' ye;
An' a' the folk on a' the way
      Were blithe to see ye.

O sir, the gods are kind indeed,
An' hauld ye for an honoured heid,
That for a wee bit clarkit screed
  Sae weel reward ye,
An' lend – puir Rabbie bein' deid –
  His ghaist to guard ye.

For though, whaure'er yoursel' may be,
We've just to turn an' glisk a wee,
An' Rab at heel we're shüre to see
  Wi' gladsome caper:
The bogle of a bogle, he –
  A ghaist o' paper!

And as the auld-farrand hero sees
In Hell a bogle Hercules,
Pit there the lesser deid to please,
  While he himsel'
Dwalls wi' the muckle gods at ease
  Far raised frae hell:

Sae the true Rabbie far has gane
On kindlier business o' his ain
Wi' aulder frien's; an' his breist-bane
  An' stumpie tailie,
He birstles at a new hearth stane
  By James and Ailie.

XVI 'It's an owercome sooth for age an' youth'

It's an owercome sooth for age an' youth
  And it brooks wi' nae denial,
That the dearest friends are the auldest friends
  And the young are just on trial.

There's a rival bauld wi' young an' auld
   And it's him that has bereft me;
For the sürest friends are the auldest friends
   And the maist o' mines hae left me.

There are kind hearts still, for friends to fill
10   And fools to take and break them;
But the nearest friends are the auldest friends
   And the grave's the place to seek them.

FROM *BALLADS* (1890)

The Song of Rahéro

A LEGEND OF TAHITI

TO ORI A ORI
Ori, my brother in the island mode,
In every tongue and meaning much my friend,
This story of your country and your clan,
In your loved house, your too much honoured guest,
I made in English. Take it, being done;
And let me sign it with the name you gave.

TERIITERA

I THE SLAYING OF TÁMATÉA

It fell in the days of old, as the men of Taiárapu tell,
A youth went forth to the fishing, and fortune favoured
him well.
Támatéa his name: gullible, simple, and kind,
Comely of countenance, nimble of body, empty of mind,
His mother ruled him and loved him beyond the wont of a
wife,
Serving the lad for eyes and living herself in his life.

Alone from the sea and the fishing came Támatéa the fair,
Urging his boat to the beach, and the mother awaited him
there,
— 'Long may you live!' said she. 'Your fishing has sped to a
wish.
And now let us choose for the king the fairest of all your
fish.
For fear inhabits the palace and grudging grows in the land,
Marked is the sluggardly foot and marked the niggardly
hand,
The hours and the miles are counted, the tributes
numbered and weighed,
And woe to him that comes short, and woe to him that
delayed!'

So spoke on the beach the mother, and counselled the wiser
    thing.
For Rahéro stirred in the country and secretly mined the
    king.
Nor were the signals wanting of how the leaven wrought,
In the cords of obedience loosed and the tributes
    grudgingly brought.
And when last to the temple of Oro the boat with the
    victim sped,
And the priest uncovered the basket and looked on the face
    of the dead,
Trembling fell upon all at sight of an ominous thing,
For there was the aito dead, and he of the house of the
    king.

So spake on the beach the mother, matter worthy of note,
30 And wattled a basket well, and chose a fish from the boat;
And Támatéa the pliable shouldered the basket and went,
And travelled, and sang as he travelled, a lad that was well
    content.
Still the way of his going was round by the roaring coast,
Where the ring of the reef is broke and the trades run riot
    the most.
On his left, with smoke as of battle, the billows battered the
    land;
Unscalable, turreted mountains rose on the inner hand.
And cape, and village, and river, and vale, and mountain
    above,
Each had a name in the land for men to remember and
    love;
And never the name of a place, but lo! a song in its praise;
40 Ancient and unforgotten, songs of the earlier days,
That the elders taught to the young, and at night, in the
    full of the moon,
Garlanded boys and maidens sang together in tune.
Támatéa the placable went with a lingering foot;
He sang as loud as a bird, he whistled hoarse as a flute;

He broiled in the sun, he breathed in the grateful shadow of
     trees,
In the icy stream of the rivers he waded over the knees;
And still in his empty mind crowded, a thousand-fold,
The deeds of the strong and the songs of the cunning
     heroes of old.

And now was he come to a place Taiárapu honoured the
     most,
Where a silent valley of woods debouched on the noisy
50   coast,
Spewing a level river. There was a haunt of Pai.
There, in his potent youth, when his parents drove him to
     die,
Honoura lived like a beast, lacking the lamp and the fire,
Washed by the rains of the trade and clotting his hair in the
     mire;
And there, so mighty his hands, he bent the tree to his
     foot –
So keen the spur of his hunger, he plucked it naked of
     fruit.
There, as she pondered the clouds for the shadow of
     coming ills,
Ahupu, the woman of song, walked on high on the hills.

Of these was Rahéro sprung, a man of a godly race;
And inherited cunning of spirit and beauty of body and
60   face.
Of yore in his youth, as an aito, Rahéro wandered the land,
Delighting maids with his tongue, smiting men with his
     hand.
Famous he was in his youth; but before the midst of his life
Paused, and fashioned a song of farewell to glory and strife.

> *House of mine (it went), house upon the sea,*
> *Belov'd of all my fathers, more belov'd by me!*
> *Vale of the strong Honoura, deep ravine of Pai,*
> *Again in your woody summits I hear the trade-wind cry.*

> *House of mine, in your walls, strong sounds the sea,*
70   *Of all sounds on earth, dearest sound to me.*
> *I have heard the applause of men, I have heard it arise*
> *and die:*
> *Sweeter now in my house I hear the trade-wind cry.*

These were the words of his singing, other the thought of
    his heart;
For secret desire of glory vexed him, dwelling apart.
Lazy and crafty he was, and loved to lie in the sun,
And loved the cackle of talk and the true word uttered in
    fun;
Lazy he was, his roof was ragged, his table was lean,
And the fish swam safe in his sea, and he gathered the near
    and the green.
He sat in his house and laughed, but he loathed the king of
    the land,
And he uttered the grudging word under the covering
80   hand.
Treason spread from his door; and he looked for a day to
    come,
A day of the crowding people, a day of the summoning
    drum,
When the vote should be taken, the king be driven forth in
    disgrace,
And Rahéro, the laughing and lazy, sit and rule in his place.

Here Támatéa came, and beheld the house on the brook;
And Rahéro was there by the way and covered an oven to
    cook.
Naked he was to the loins, but the tattoo covered the lack,
And the sun and the shadow of palms dappled his muscular
    back.
Swiftly he lifted his head at the fall of the coming feet,
And the water sprang in his mouth with a sudden desire of
90   meat;

For he marked the basket carried, covered from flies and
    the sun;
And Rahéro buried his fire, but the meat in his house was
    done.

Forth he stepped; and took, and delayed the boy, by the
    hand;
And vaunted the joys of meat and the ancient ways of the
    land:
– 'Our sires of old in Taiárapu, they that created the race,
Ate ever with eager hand, nor regarded season or place,
Ate in the boat at the oar, on the way afoot; and at night
Arose in the midst of dreams to rummage the house for a
    bite.
It is good for the youth in his turn to follow the way of the
    sire;
And behold how fitting the time! for here do I cover my
100   fire.'
– 'I see the fire for the cooking but never the meat to cook,'
Said Támatéa. – 'Tut!' said Rahéro. 'Here in the brook
And there in the tumbling sea, the fishes are thick as flies,
Hungry like healthy men, and like pigs for savour and size:
Crayfish crowding the river, sea-fish thronging the sea.'
— 'Well it may be,' said the other, 'and yet be nothing to
    me.
Fain would I eat, but alas! I have needful matter in hand,
Since I carry my tribute of fish to the jealous king of the
    land.'

Now at the word a light sprang in Rahéro's eyes.
'I will gain me a dinner,' thought he, 'and lend the king a
110   surprise.'
And he took the lad by the arm, as they stood by the side of
    the track,
And smiled, and rallied, and flattered, and pushed him
    forward and back.

It was 'You that sing like a bird, I never have heard you
    sing,'
And 'The lads when I was a lad were none so feared of a
    king.
And of what account is an hour, when the heart is empty of
    guile?
But come, and sit in the house and laugh with the women
    awhile;
And I will but drop my hook, and behold! the dinner
    made.'

So Támatéa the pliable hung up his fish in the shade
On a tree by the side of the way; and Rahéro carried him
    in,
Smiling as smiles the fowler when flutters the bird to the
120   gin,
And chose him a shining hook, and viewed it with sedulous
    eye,
And breathed and burnished it well on the brawn of his
    naked thigh,
And set a mat for the gull, and bade him be merry and
    bide,
Like a man concerned for his guest, and the fishing, and
    nothing beside.

Now when Rahéro was forth, he paused and hearkened,
    and heard
The gull jest in the house and the women laugh at his
    word;
And stealthily crossed to the side of the way, to the shady
    place
Where the basket hung on a mango; and craft transfigured
    his face.
Deftly he opened the basket, and took of the fat of the fish,
130 The cut of kings and chieftains, enough for a goodly dish.
This he wrapped in a leaf, set on the fire to cook
And buried; and next the marred remains of the tribute he
    took,

And doubled and packed them well, and covered the basket
   close
— 'There is a buffet, my king,' quoth he, 'and a nauseous
   dose!' —
And hung the basket again in the shade, in a cloud of flies
— 'And there is a sauce to your dinner, king of the crafty
   eyes!'

Soon as the oven was open, the fish smelt excellent good.
In the shade, by the house of Rahéro, down they sat to
   their food,
And cleared the leaves in silence, or uttered a jest and
   laughed,
And raising the cocoanut bowls, buried their faces and
140   quaffed.
But chiefly in silence they ate; and soon as the meal was
   done,
Rahéro feigned to remember and measured the hour by the
   sun,
And 'Támatéa,' quoth he, 'it is time to be jogging, my lad.'

So Támatéa arose, doing ever the thing he was bade,
And carelessly shouldered the basket, and kindly saluted his
   host;
And again the way of his going was round by the roaring
   coast.
Long he went; and at length was aware of a pleasant green,
And the stems and shadows of palms, and roofs of lodges
   between
There sate, in the door of his palace, the king on a kingly
   seat,
And aitos stood armed around, and the yottowas sat at his
150   feet.
But fear was a worm in his heart: fear darted his eyes;
And he probed men's faces for treasons and pondered their
   speech for lies.
To him came Támatéa, the basket slung in his hand,
And paid him the due obeisance standing as vassals stand.

In silence hearkened the king, and closed the eyes in his
    face,
Harbouring odious thoughts and the baseless fears of the
    base;
In silence accepted the gift and sent the giver away.
So Támatéa departed, turning his back on the day.

And lo! as the king sat brooding, a rumour rose in the
    crowd;
The yottowas nudged and whispered, the commons
160   murmured aloud;
Tittering fell upon all at sight of the impudent thing,
At the sight of a gift unroyal flung in the face of a king.
And the face of the king turned white and red with anger
    and shame
In their midst; and the heart in his body was water and
    then was flame;
Till of a sudden, turning, he gripped an aito hard,
A youth that stood with his ómare, one of the daily guard,
And spat in his ear a command, and pointed and uttered a
    name,
And hid in the shade of the house his impotent anger and
    shame.

Now Tamatéa the fool was far on the homeward way,
170   The rising night in his face, behind him the dying day.
Rahéro saw him go by, and the heart of Rahéro was glad,
Devising shame to the king and nowise harm to the lad;
And all that dwelt by the way saw and saluted him well,
For he had the face of a friend and the news of the town to
    tell;
And pleased with the notice of folk, and pleased that his
    journey was done,
Támatéa drew homeward, turning his back to the sun.

And now was the hour of the bath in Taiárapu: far and near
The lovely laughter of bathers rose and delighted his ear.

Night massed in the valleys; the sun on the mountain coast
Struck, end-long; and above the clouds embattled their
180   host,
And glowed and gloomed on the heights; and the heads of
      the palms were gems,
And far to the rising eve extended the shade of their stems;
And the shadow of Támatéa hovered already at home.

And sudden the sound of one coming and running light as
      the foam
Struck on his ear; and he turned, and lo! a man on his
      track,
Girded and armed with an ómare, following hard at his
      back.
At a bound the man was upon him; – and, or ever a word
      was said,
The loaded end of the ómare fell and laid him dead.

II THE VENGING OF TÁMATÉA

Thus was Rahéro's treason; thus and no further it sped.
190 The king sat safe in his place and a kindly fool was dead.

But the mother of Támatéa arose with death in her eyes.
All night long, and the next, Taiárapu rang with her cries.
As when a babe in the wood turns with a chill of doubt
And perceives nor home, nor friends, for the trees have
      closed her about,
The mountain rings and her breast is torn with the voice of
      despair:
So the lion-like woman idly wearied the air
For awhile, and pierced men's hearing in vain, and
      wounded their hearts.
But as when the weather changes at sea, in dangerous parts,
And sudden the hurricane wrack unrolls up the front of the
      sky,
200 At once the ship lies idle, the sails hang silent on high,

The breath of the wind that blew is blown out like the
    flame of a lamp,
And the silent armies of death draw near with inaudible
    tramp:
So sudden, the voice of her weeping ceased; in silence she
    rose
And passed from the house of her sorrow, a woman clothed
    with repose,
Carrying death in her breast and sharpening death with her
    hand.

Hither she went and thither in all the coasts of the land.
They tell that she feared not to slumber alone, in the dead
    of night,
In accursed places; beheld, unblenched, the ribbon of light
Spin from temple to temple; guided the perilous skiff,
Abhorred not the paths of the mountain and trod the verge
210   of the cliff;
From end to end of the island, thought not the distance
    long,
But forth from king to king carried the tale of her wrong.
To king after king, as they sat in the palace door, she came,
Claiming kinship, declaiming verses, naming her name
And the names of all of her fathers; and still, with a heart
    on the rack,
Jested to capture a hearing and laughed when they jested
    back:
So would deceive them awhile, and change and return in a
    breath,
And on all the men of Vaiau imprecate instant death;
And tempt her kings – for Vaiau was a rich and prosperous
    land,
And flatter – for who would attempt it but warriors mighty
220   of hand?
And change in a breath again and rise in a strain of song,
Invoking the beaten drums, beholding the fall of the strong,
Calling the fowls of the air to come and feast on the dead.
And they held the chin in silence, and heard her, and shook
    the head;

For they knew the men of Taiárapu famous in battle and
    feast,
Marvellous eaters and smiters: the men of Vaiau not least.

To the land of the Námunu-úra, to Paea, at length she
    came,
To men who were foes to the Tevas and hated their race
    and name.
There was she well received, and spoke with Hiopa the
    king.
And Hiopa listened, and weighed, and wisely considered
230   the thing.
'Here in the back of the isle we dwell in a sheltered place,'
Quoth he to the woman, 'in quiet, a weak and peaceable
    race.
But far in the teeth of the wind lofty Taiárapu lies;
Strong blows the wind of the trade on its seaward face, and
    cries,
Aloud in the top of arduous mountains, and utters its song
In green continuous forests. Strong is the wind, and strong
And fruitful and hardy the race, famous in battle and feast,
Marvellous eaters and smiters: the men of Vaiau not least.
Now hearken to me, my daughter, and hear a word of the
    wise:
How a strength goes linked with a weakness, two by two,
240   like the eyes.
They can wield the ómare well and cast the javelin far;
Yet are they greedy and weak as the swine and the children
    are.
Plant we, then, here at Paea, a garden of excellent fruits;
Plant we bananas and kava and taro, the king of roots;
Let the pigs in Paea be tapu and no man fish for a year;
And of all the meat in Tahiti gather we threefold here.
So shall the fame of our plenty fill the island, and so,
At last, on the tongue of rumour, go where we wish it to
    go.
Then shall the pigs of Taiárapu raise their snouts in the air;
250   But we sit quiet and wait, as the fowler sits by the snare,

And tranquilly fold our hands, till the pigs come nosing the
     food:
But meanwhile build us a house of Trotéa, the stubborn
     wood,
Bind it with incombustible thongs, set a roof to the room,
Too strong for the hands of a man to dissever or fire to
     consume;
And there, when the pigs come trotting, there shall the
     feast be spread,
There shall the eye of the morn enlighten the feasters dead.
So be it done; for I have a heart that pities your state,
And Nateva and Námunu-úra are fire and water for hate.'

All was done as he said, and the gardens prospered; and
     now
The fame of their plenty went out, and word of it came to
260   Vaiau.
For the men of Námunu-úra sailed, to the windward far,
Lay in the offing by south where the towns of the Tevas
     are,
And cast overboard of their plenty; and lo! at the Tevas'
     feet
The surf on all of the beaches tumbled treasures of meat.
In the salt of the sea, a harvest tossed with the refluent
     foam;
And the children gleaned it in playing, and ate and carried
     it home;
And the elders stared and debated, and wondered and
     passed the jest,
But whenever a guest came by eagerly questioned the guest;
And little by little, from one to another, the word went
     round:
270 'In all the borders of Paea the victual rots on the ground,
And swine are plenty as rats. And now, when they fare to
     the sea,
The men of the Námunu-úra glean from under the tree
And load the canoe to the gunwale with all that is
     toothsome to eat;
And all day long on the sea the jaws are crushing the meat,

The steersman eats at the helm, the rowers munch at the
    oar,
And at length, when their bellies are full, overboard with
    the store!'
Now was the word made true, and soon as the bait was
    bare,
All the pigs of Taiárapu raised their snouts in the air.
Songs were recited, and kinship was counted, and tales
    were told
280   How war had severed of late but peace had cemented of old
The clans of the island. 'To war,' said they, 'now set we an
    end,
And hie to the Námunu-úra even as a friend to a friend.'

So judged, and a day was named; and soon as the morning
    broke,
Canoes were thrust in the sea and the houses emptied of
    folk.
Strong blew the wind of the south, the wind that gathers
    the clan;
Along all the line of the reef the clamorous surges ran;
And the clouds were piled on the top of the island
    mountain-high,
A mountain throned on a mountain. The fleet of canoes
    swept by
In the midst, on the green lagoon, with a crew released
    from care,
290   Sailing an even water, breathing a summer air,
Cheered by a cloudless sun; and ever to left and right,
Bursting surge on the reef, drenching storms on the height.
So the folk of Vaiau sailed and were glad all day,
Coasting the palm-tree cape and crossing the populous bay
By all the towns of the Tevas; and still as they bowled
    along,
Boat would answer to boat with jest and laughter and song,
And the people of all the towns trooped to the sides of the
    sea
And gazed from under the hand or sprang aloft on the tree,

Hailing and cheering. Time failed them for more to do;
The holiday village careened to the wind, and was gone
300   from view
Swift as a passing bird; and ever as onward it bore,
Like the cry of the passing bird, bequeathed its song to the
      shore –
Desirable laughter of maids and the cry of delight of the
      child.
And the gazer, left behind, stared at the wake and smiled.

By all the towns of the Tevas they went, and Pápara last,
The home of the chief, the place of muster in war; and
      passed
The march of the lands of the clan, to the lands of an alien
      folk.
And there, from the dusk of the shoreside palms, a column
      of smoke
Mounted and wavered and died in the gold of the setting
      sun,
310   'Paea!' they cried. 'It is Paea.' And so was the voyage done.

In the early fall of the night, Hiopa came to the shore,
And beheld and counted the comers, and lo, they were
      forty score:
The pelting feet of the babes that ran already and played,
The clean-lipped smile of the boy, the slender breasts of
      the maid,
And mighty limbs of women, stalwart mothers of men.
The sires stood forth unabashed; but a little back from his
      ken
Clustered the scarcely nubile, the lads and maids, in a ring,
Fain of each other, afraid of themselves, aware of the king
And aping behaviour, but clinging together with hands and
      eyes,
With looks that were kind like kisses, and laughter tender
320   as sighs.
There, too, the grandsire stood, raising his silver crest,
And the impotent hands of a suckling groped in his barren
      breast.

The childhood of love, the pair well married, the innocent
   brood,
The tale of the generations repeated and ever renewed –
Hiopa beheld them together, all the ages of man,
And a moment shook in his purpose.

                        But these were the foes of his clan,
And he trod upon pity, and came, and civilly greeted the
   king,
And gravely entreated Rahéro; and for all that could fight
   or sing,
And claimed a name in the land, had fitting phrases of
   praise;
But with all who were well-descended he spoke of the
330   ancient days.
And ' 'Tis true,' said he, 'that in Paea the victual rots on
   the ground;
But, friends, your number is many; and pigs must be
   hunted and found,
And the lads troop to the mountains to bring the féis down,
And around the bowls of the kava cluster the maids of the
   town.
So, for to-night, sleep here; but king, common, and priest
To-morrow, in order due, shall sit with me in the feast.'
Sleepless the live-long night, Hiopa's followers toiled.
The pigs screamed and were slaughtered; the spars of the
   guest-house oiled,
The leaves spread on the floor. In many a mountain glen
The moon drew shadows of trees on the naked bodies of
340   men
Plucking and bearing fruits; and in all the bounds of the
   town
Red glowed the cocoanut fires, and were buried and
   trodden down.
Thus did seven of the yottowas toil with their tale of the
   clan,
But the eighth wrought with his lads, hid from the sight of
   man.

In the deeps of the woods they laboured, piling the fuel
    high
In faggots, the load of a man, fuel seasoned and dry,
Thirsty to seize upon fire and apt to blurt into flame.

And now was the day of the feast. The forests, as morning
    came,
Tossed in the wind, and the peaks quaked in the blaze of
    the day
And the cocoanuts showered on the ground, rebounding
350   and rolling away:
A glorious morn for a feast, a famous wind for a fire.
To the hall of feasting Hiopa led them, mother and sire
And maid and babe in a tale, the whole of the holiday
    throng.
Smiling they came, garlanded green, not dreaming of
    wrong;
And for every three, a pig, tenderly cooked in the ground,
Waited; and féi, the staff of life, heaped in a mound
For each where he sat; – for each, bananas roasted and raw
Piled with a bountiful hand, as for horses hay and straw
Are stacked in a stable; and fish, the food of desire,
And plentiful vessels of sauce, and breadfruit gilt in the
360   fire;
And kava was common as water. Feasts have there been ere
    now,
And many, but never a feast like that of the folk of Vaiau.

All day long they ate with the resolute greed of brutes,
And turned from the pigs to the fish, and again from the
    fish to the fruits,
And emptied the vessels of sauce, and drank of the kava
    deep;
Till the young lay stupid as stones, and the strongest
    nodded to sleep.
Sleep that was mighty as death and blind as a moonless
    night
Tethered them hand and foot; and their souls were
    drowned, and the light

Was cloaked from their eyes. Senseless together, the old
    and the young,
The fighter deadly to smite and the prater cunning of
370   tongue,
The woman wedded and fruitful, inured to the pangs of
    birth,
And the maid that knew not of kisses, blindly sprawled on
    the earth.

From the hall Hiopa the king and his chiefs came stealthily
    forth.
Already the sun hung low and enlightened the peaks of the
    north;
But the wind was stubborn to die and blew as it blows at
    morn,
Showering the nuts in the dusk, and e'en as a banner is
    torn,
High on the peaks of the island, shattered the mountain
    cloud.
And now at once, at a signal, a silent, emulous crowd
Set hands to the work of death, hurrying to and fro,
Like ants, to furnish the faggots, building them broad and
380   low,
And piling them high and higher around the walls of the
    hall.
Silence persisted within, for sleep lay heavy on all;
But the mother of Támatéa stood at Hiopa's side,
And shook for terror and joy like a girl that is a bride.
Night fell on the toilers, and first Hiopa the wise
Made the round of the house, visiting all with his eyes;
And all was piled to the eaves, and fuel blockaded the door;
And within, in the house beleaguered, slumbered the forty
    score.
Then was an aito dispatched and came with fire in his
    hand,
390 And Hiopa took it. — 'Within', said he, 'is the life of a land;
And behold! I breathe on the coal, I breathe on the dales of
    the east,
And silence falls on forest and shore; the voice of the feast

Is quenched, and the smoke of cooking; the rooftree decays
    and falls
On the empty lodge, and the winds subvert deserted walls.'

Therewithal, to the fuel, he laid the glowing coal;
And the redness ran in the mass and burrowed within like a
    mole,
And copious smoke was conceived. But, as when a dam is
    to burst,
The water lips it and crosses in silver trickles at first,
And then, of a sudden, whelms and bears it away
    forthright:
So now, in a moment, the flame sprang and towered in the
400   night,
And wrestled and roared in the wind, and high over house
    and tree,
Stood, like a streaming torch, enlightening land and sea.

But the mother of Támatéa threw her arms abroad,
'Pyre of my son,' she shouted, 'debited vengeance of God,
Late, late, I behold you, yet I behold you at last,
And glory, beholding! For now are the days of my agony
    past,
The lust that famished my soul now eats and drinks its
    desire,
And they that encompassed my son shrivel alive in the fire.
Tenfold precious the vengeance that comes after lingering
    years!
Ye quenched the voice of my singer? – hark, in your dying
410   ears,
The song of the conflagration! Ye left me a widow alone?
– Behold, the whole of your race consumes, sinew and bone
And torturing flesh together: man, mother, and maid
Heaped in a common shambles; and already, borne by the
    trade,
The smoke of your dissolution darkens the stars of night.'

Thus she spoke, and her stature grew in the people's sight.

III RAHÉRO

Rahéro was there in the hall asleep: beside him his wife,
Comely, a mirthful woman, one that delighted in life;
And a girl that was ripe for marriage, shy and sly as a
    mouse;
420   And a boy, a climber of trees: all the hopes of his house.
Unwary, with open hands, he slept in the midst of his
    folk,
And dreamed that he heard a voice crying without, and
    awoke,
Leaping blindly afoot like one from a dream that he fears.
A hellish glow and clouds were about him; — it roared in his
    ears
Like the sound of the cataract fall that plunges sudden and
    steep;
And Rahéro swayed as he stood, and his reason was still
    asleep.
Now the flame struck hard on the house, wind-wielded, a
    fracturing blow,
And the end of the roof was burst and fell on the sleepers
    below;
And the lofty hall, and the feast, and the prostrate bodies of
    folk,
Shone red in his eyes a moment, and then were swallowed
430   of smoke.
In the mind of Rahéro clearness came; and he opened his
    throat;
And as when a squall comes sudden, the straining sail of a
    boat
Thunders aloud and bursts, so thundered the voice of the
    man.
— 'The wind and the rain!' he shouted, the mustering word
    of the clan,
And 'up!' and 'to arms, men of Vaiau!' But silence replied,
Or only the voice of the gusts of the fire, and nothing
    beside.

Rahéro stooped and groped. He handled his womankind,
But the fumes of the fire and the kava had quenched the
    life of their mind,
And they lay like pillars prone; and his hand encountered
    the boy,
And there sprang in the gloom of his soul a sudden
440   lightning of joy.
'Him can I save!' he thought, 'if I were speedy enough.'
And he loosened the cloth from his loins, and swaddled the
    child in the stuff;
And about the strength of his neck he knotted the burden
    well.

There where the roof had fallen, it roared like the mouth of
    hell.
Thither Rahéro went, stumbling on senseless folk,
And grappled a post of the house, and began to climb in
    the smoke:
The last alive of Vaiau; and the son borne by the sire.
The post glowed in the grain with ulcers of eating fire,
And the fire bit to the blood and mangled his hands and
    thighs;
And the fumes sang in his head like wine and stung in his
450   eyes;
And still he climbed, and came to the top, the place of
    proof,
And thrust a hand through the flame, and clambered alive
    on the roof.
But even as he did so, the wind, in a garment of flames and
    pain,
Wrapped him from head to heel; and the waistcloth parted
    in twain;
And the living fruit of his loins dropped in the fire below.

About the blazing feast-house clustered the eyes of the foe,
Watching, hand upon weapon, lest ever a soul should flee,
Shading the brow from the glare, straining the neck to see.

Only, to leeward, the flames in the wind swept far and
    wide,
And the forest sputtered on fire; and there might no man
460   abide.
Thither Rahéro crept, and dropped from the burning eaves,
And crouching low to the ground, in a treble covert of
    leaves
And fire and volleying smoke, ran for the life of his soul
Unseen; and behind him under a furnace of ardent coal,
Cairned with a wonder of flame, and blotting the night with
    smoke,
Blazed and were smelted together the bones of all his folk.

He fled unguided at first; but hearing the breakers roar,
Thitherward shaped his way, and came at length to the
    shore.
Sound-limbed he was: dry-eyed; but smarted in every part;
And the mighty cage of his ribs heaved on his straining
470   heart
With sorrow and rage. And 'Fools!' he cried, 'fools of
    Vaiau,
Heads of swine – gluttons – Alas! and where are they now?
Those that I played with, those that nursed me, those that I
    nursed?
God, and I outliving them! I, the least and the worst –
I, that thought myself crafty, snared by this herd of swine,
In the tortures of hell and desolate, stripped of all that was
    mine:
All! – my friends and my fathers – the silver heads of yore
That trooped to the council, the children that ran to the
    open door
Crying with innocent voices and clasping a father's knees!
And mine, my wife – my daughter – my sturdy climber of
480   trees,
Ah, never to climb again!'

            Thus in the dusk of the night
(For clouds rolled in the sky and the moon was swallowed
    from sight),

Pacing and gnawing his fists, Rahéro raged by the shore.
Vengeance: that must be his. But much was to do before;
And first a single life to be snatched from a deadly place,
A life, the root of revenge, surviving plant of the race:
And next the race to be raised anew, and the lands of the
   clan
Repeopled. So Rahéro designed, a prudent man
Even in wrath, and turned for the means of revenge and
   escape:
490   A boat to be seized by stealth, a wife to be taken by rape.

Still was the dark lagoon; beyond on the coral wall,
He saw the breakers shine, he heard them bellow and fall.
Alone, on the top of the reef, a man with a flaming brand
Walked, gazing and pausing, a fish-spear poised in his
   hand.
The foam boiled to his calf when the mightier breakers
   came,
And the torch shed in the wind scattering tufts of flame.
Afar on the dark lagoon a canoe lay idly at wait:
A figure dimly guiding it: surely the fisherman's mate.
Rahéro saw and he smiled. He straightened his mighty
   thews:
Naked, with never a weapon, and covered with scorch and
500   bruise,
He straightened his arms, he filled the void of his body
   with breath,
And, strong as the wind in his manhood, doomed the fisher
   to death.

Silent he entered the water, and silently swam, and came
There where the fisher walked, holding on high the flame.
Loud on the pier of the reef volleyed the breach of the sea;
And hard at the back of the man, Rahéro crept to his knee
On the coral, and suddenly sprang and seized him, the
   elder hand
Clutching the joint of his throat, the other snatching the
   brand

Ere it had time to fall, and holding it steady and high.
510   Strong was the fisher, brave, and swift of mind and of eye –
Strongly he threw in the clutch; but Rahéro resisted the
    strain,
And jerked, and the spine of life snapped with a crack in
    twain,
And the man came slack in his hands and tumbled a lump
    at his feet.

One moment: and there, on the reef, where the breakers
    whitened and beat,
Rahéro was standing alone, glowing and scorched and bare,
A victor unknown of any, raising the torch in the air.
But once he drank of his breath, and instantly set him to
    fish
Like a man intent upon supper at home and a savoury dish.
For what should the woman have seen? A man with a torch
    – and then
A moment's blur of the eyes – and a man with a torch
520   again.
And the torch had scarcely been shaken. 'Ah, surely,'
    Rahéro said,
'She will deem it a trick of the eyes, a fancy born in the
    head;
But time must be given the fool to nourish a fool's belief.'
So for a while, a sedulous fisher, he walked the reef,
Pausing at times and gazing, striking at times with the
    spear:
– Lastly, uttered the call; and even as the boat drew near,
Like a man that was done with its use, tossed the torch in
    the sea.

Lightly he leaped on the boat beside the woman; and she
Lightly addressed him, and yielded the paddle and place to
    sit;
For now the torch was extinguished the night was black as
530   the pit.
Rahéro set him to row, never a word he spoke,
And the boat sang in the water urged by his vigorous
    stroke.

– 'What ails you?' the woman asked, 'and why did you drop
  the brand?
We have only to kindle another as soon as we come to
  land.'
Never a word Rahéro replied, but urged the canoe.
And a chill fell on the woman. – 'Atta! speak! is it you?
Speak! Why are you silent? Why do you bend aside?
Wherefore steer to the seaward?' thus she panted and cried.
Never a word from the oarsman, toiling there in the dark;
540 But right for a gate of the reef he silently headed the bark,
And wielding the single paddle with passionate sweep on
  sweep,
Drove her, the little fitted, forth on the open deep.

And fear, there where she sat, froze the woman to stone:
Not fear of the crazy boat and the weltering deep alone;
But a keener fear of the night, the dark, and the ghostly
  hour,
And the thing that drove the canoe with more than a
  mortal's power
And more than a mortal's boldness. For much she knew of
  the dead
That haunt and fish upon reefs, toiling, like men, for bread,
And traffic with human fishers, or slay them and take their
  ware,
Till the hour when the star of the dead goes down, and the
550 morning air
Blows, and the cocks are singing on shore. And surely she
  knew
The speechless thing at her side belonged to the grave.

                                              It blew
All night from the south; all night, Rahéro contended and
  kept
The prow to the cresting sea; and, silent as though she
  slept,
The woman huddled and quaked. And now was the peep of
  day.
High and long on their left the mountainous island lay;

And over the peaks of Taiárapu arrows of sunlight struck.
On shore the birds were beginning to sing: the ghostly
    ruck
Of the buried had long ago returned to the covered grave;
560 And here on the sea, the woman, waxing suddenly brave,
Turned her swiftly about and looked in the face of the
    man.
And sure he was none that she knew, none of her country
    or clan:
A stranger, mother-naked, and marred with the marks of
    fire,
But comely and great of stature, a man to obey and admire.

And Rahéro regarded her also, fixed, with a frowning face,
Judging the woman's fitness to mother a warlike race.
Broad of shoulder, ample of girdle, long in the thigh,
Deep of bosom she was, and bravely supported his eye.

'Woman,' said he, 'last night the men of your folk –
570 Man, woman, and maid, smothered my race in smoke.
It was done like cowards; and I, a mighty man of my
    hands,
Escaped, a single life; and now to the empty lands
And smokeless hearths of my people, sail, with yourself,
    alone.
Before your mother was born, the die of to-day was thrown
And you selected: – your husband, vainly striving, to fall
Broken between these hands: – yourself to be severed from
    all,
The places, the people, you love – home, kindred, and
    clan –
And to dwell in a desert and bear the babes of a kinless
    man.'

Ticonderoga

A LEGEND OF THE WEST HIGHLANDS

This is the tale of the man
    Who heard a word in the night
In the land of the heathery hills,
    In the days of the feud and the fight.
By the sides of the rainy sea,
    Where never a stranger came,
On the awful lips of the dead,
    He heard the outlandish name.
It sang in his sleeping ears,
10   It hummed in his waking head:
The name – Ticonderoga,
    The utterance of the dead.

I THE SAYING OF THE NAME

On the loch-sides of Appin,
    When the mist blew from the sea,
A Stewart stood with a Cameron:
    An angry man was he.
The blood beat in his ears,
    The blood ran hot to his head,
The mist blew from the sea,
20   And there was the Cameron dead.

'O, what have I done to my friend,
    O, what have I done to mysel',
That he should be cold and dead,
    And I in the danger of all?
Nothing but danger about me.
    Danger behind and before,
Death at wait in the heather
    In Appin and Mamore,
Hate at all of the ferries
30   And death at each of the fords,
Camerons priming gunlocks
    And Camerons sharpening swords.'

But this was a man of counsel,
    This was a man of a score,
There dwelt no pawkier Stewart
    In Appin or Mamore.
He looked on the blowing mist,
    He looked on the awful dead,
And there came a smile on his face
40   And there slipped a thought in his head.

Out over cairn and moss,
    Out over scrog and scaur,
He ran as runs the clansman
    That bears the cross of war.
His heart beat in his body,
    His hair clove to his face,
When he came at last in the gloaming
    To the dead man's brother's place.
The east was white with the moon,
50   The west with the sun was red,
And there, in the house-doorway,
    Stood the brother of the dead.

'I have slain a man to my danger,
    I have slain a man to my death.
I put my soul in your hands,'
    The panting Stewart saith.
'I lay it bare in your hands,
    For I know your hands are leal;
And be you my targe and bulwark
60   From the bullet and the steel.'
Then up and spoke the Cameron,
    And gave him his hand again:
'There shall never a man in Scotland
    Set faith in me in vain;
And whatever man you have slaughtered,
    Of whatever name or line,
By my sword and yonder mountain,
    I make your quarrel mine.
I bid you in to my fireside,

70   I share with you house and hall;
    It stands upon my honour
        To see you safe from all.'

    It fell in the time of midnight,
        When the fox barked in the den
    And the plaids were over the faces
        In all the houses of men,
    That as the living Cameron
        Lay sleepless on his bed,
    Out of the night and the other world,
80   Came in to him the dead.

    'My blood is on the heather,
        My bones are on the hill;
    There is joy in the home of ravens
        That the young shall eat their fill.
    My blood is poured in the dust,
        My soul is spilled in the air;
    And the man that has undone me
        Sleeps in my brother's care.'

    'I'm wae for your death, my brother,
90   But if all of my house were dead,
    I couldnae withdraw the plighted hand,
        Nor break the word once said.'

    'O, what shall I say to our father,
        In the place to which I fare?
    O, what shall I say to our mother,
        Who greets to see me there?
    And to all the kindly Camerons
        That have lived and died long-syne –
    Is this the word you send them,
100   Fause-hearted brother mine?'

    'It's neither fear nor duty,
        It's neither quick nor dead
    Shall gar me withdraw the plighted hand,
        Or break the word once said.'

Thrice in the time of midnight,
   When the fox barked in the den,
And the plaids were over the faces
   In all the houses of men,
Thrice as the living Cameron
110   Lay sleepless on his bed,
Out of the night and the other world
   Came in to him the dead,
And cried to him for vengeance
   On the man that laid him low;
And thrice the living Cameron
   Told the dead Cameron, no.

'Thrice have you seen me, brother,
   But now shall see me no more,
Till you meet your angry fathers
120   Upon the farther shore.
Thrice have I spoken, and now,
   Before the cock be heard,
I take my leave for ever
   With the naming of a word.
It shall sing in your sleeping ears,
   It shall hum in your waking head,
The name – Ticonderoga,
   And the warning of the dead.'

Now when the night was over
130   And the time of people's fears,
The Cameron walked abroad,
   And the word was in his ears.
'Many a name I know,
   But never a name like this;
O, where shall I find a skilly man
   Shall tell me what it is?'
With many a man he counselled
   Of high and low degree,
With the herdsmen on the mountains
140   And the fishers of the sea.
And he came and went unweary,

And read the books of yore,
And the runes that were written of old
   On stones upon the moor.
And many a name he was told,
   But never the name of his fears –
Never, in east or west,
   The name that rang in his ears:
Names of men and of clans;
150   Names for the grass and the tree,
For the smallest tarn in the mountains,
   The smallest reef in the sea:
Names for the high and low,
   The names of the craig and the flat;
But in all the land of Scotland,
   Never a name like that.

II THE SEEKING OF THE NAME

And now there was speech in the south,
   And a man of the south that was wise,
A periwig'd lord of London,
160   Called on the clans to rise.
And the riders rode, and the summons
   Came to the western shore,
To the land of the sea and the heather,
   To Appin and Mamore.
It called on all to gather
   From every scrog and scaur,
That loved their fathers' tartan
   And the ancient game of war.
And down the watery valley
170   And up the windy hill,
Once more, as in the olden,
   The pipes were sounding shrill;
Again in highland sunshine
   The naked steel was bright;
And the lads, once more in tartan,
   Went forth again to fight.

'O, why should I dwell here
  With a weird upon my life,
When the clansmen shout for battle
180 And the war-swords clash in strife?
I cannae joy at feast,
  I cannae sleep in bed,
For the wonder of the word
  And the warning of the dead.
It sings in my sleeping ears,
  It hums in my waking head,
The name – Ticonderoga,
  The utterance of the dead.
Then up, and with the fighting men
190 To march away from here,
Till the cry of the great war-pipe
  Shall drown it in my ear!'

Where flew King George's ensign
  The plaided soldiers went:
They drew the sword in Germany,
  In Flanders pitched the tent.
The bells of foreign cities
  Rang far across the plain:
They passed the happy Rhine,
200 They drank the rapid Main.
Through Asiatic jungles
  The Tartans filed their way,
And the neighing of the warpipes
  Struck terror in Cathay.

'Many a name have I heard,' he thought,
  'In all the tongues of men,
Full many a name both here and there,
  Full many both now and then.
When I was at home in my father's house
210 In the land of the naked knee,
Between the eagles that fly in the lift
  And the herrings that swim in the sea,

And now that I am a captain-man
  With a braw cockade in my hat –
Many a name have I heard,' he thought,
  'But never a name like that.'

III THE PLACE OF THE NAME

There fell a war in a woody place,
  Lay far across the sea,
A war of the march in the mirk midnight
220   And the shot from behind the tree,
The shaven head and the painted face,
  The silent foot in the wood,
In a land of a strange, outlandish tongue
  That was hard to be understood.

It fell about the gloaming
  The general stood with his staff,
He stood and he looked east and west
  With little mind to laugh.
'Far have I been and much have I seen,
230   And kent both gain and loss,
But here we have woods on every hand
  And a kittle water to cross.
Far have I been and much have I seen,
  But never the beat of this;
And there's one must go down to that waterside
  To see how deep it is.'

It fell in the dusk of the night
  When unco things betide,
The skilly captain, the Cameron,
240   Went down to that waterside.
Canny and soft the captain went;
  And a man of the woody land,
With the shaven head and the painted face,
  Went down at his right hand.
It fell in the quiet night,

There was never a sound to ken;
But all of the woods to the right and the left
Lay filled with the painted men.

'Far have I been and much have I seen,
250   Both as a man and boy,
But never have I set forth a foot
     On so perilous an employ.'
It fell in the dusk of the night
     When unco things betide,
That he was aware of a captain-man
     Drew near to the waterside.
He was aware of his coming
     Down in the gloaming alone;
And he looked in the face of the man
260   And lo! the face was his own.
'This is my weird,' he said,
     'And now I ken the worst;
For many shall fall the morn,
     But I shall fall with the first.
O, you of the outland tongue,
     You of the painted face,
This is the place of my death;
     Can you tell me the name of the place?'
'Since the Frenchmen have been here
270   They have called it Sault-Marie;
But that is a name for priests,
     And not for you and me.
It went by another word,'
     Quoth he of the shaven head:
'It was called Ticonderoga
     In the days of the great dead.'

And it fell on the morrow's morning,
     In the fiercest of the fight,
That the Cameron bit the dust
280   As he foretold at night;
And far from the hills of heather,

Far from the isles of the sea,
He sleeps in the place of the name
As it was doomed to be.

Heather Ale

A GALLOWAY LEGEND

From the bonny bells of heather
    They brewed a drink long-syne,
Was sweeter far than honey,
    Was stronger far than wine.
They brewed it and they drank it,
    And lay in a blessed swound
For days and days together
    In their dwellings underground.

There rose a king in Scotland,
10   A fell man to his foes,
He smote the Picts in battle,
    He hunted them like roes.
Over miles of the red mountain
    He hunted as they fled,
And strewed the dwarfish bodies
    Of the dying and the dead.

Summer came in the country,
    Red was the heather bell;
But the manner of the brewing
20   Was none alive to tell.
In graves that were like children's
    On many a mountain head,
The Brewsters of the Heather
    Lay numbered with the dead.

The king in the red moorland
  Rode on a summer's day;
And the bees hummed, and the curlews
  Cried beside the way.
The king rode, and was angry,
30   Black was his brow and pale,
To rule in a land of heather
  And lack the Heather Ale.

It fortuned that his vassals,
  Riding free on the heath,
Came on a stone that was fallen
  And vermin hid beneath.
Rudely plucked from their hiding,
  Never a word they spoke:
A son and his aged father –
40   Last of the dwarfish folk.

The king sat high on his charger,
  He looked on the little men;
And the dwarfish and swarthy couple
  Looked at the king again.
Down by the shore he had them;
  And there on the giddy brink –
'I will give you life, ye vermin,
  For the secret of the drink.'

There stood the son and father
50   And they looked high and low;
The heather was red around them,
  The sea rumbled below.
And up and spoke the father,
  Shrill was his voice to hear:
'I have a word in private,
  A word for the royal ear.

'Life is dear to the aged,
  And honour a little thing;
I would gladly sell the secret,'
60   Quoth the Pict to the King.

His voice was small as a sparrow's,
    And shrill and wonderful clear:
'I would gladly sell my secret,
    Only my son I fear.

'For life is a little matter,
    And death is nought to the young;
And I dare not sell my honour
    Under the eye of my son.
Take *him*, O king, and bind him,
70   And cast him far in the deep;
And it's I will tell the secret
    That I have sworn to keep.'

They took the son and bound him
    Neck and heels in a thong,
And a lad took him and swung him,
    And flung him far and strong,
And the sea swallowed his body,
    Like that of a child of ten;
And there on the cliff stood the father,
80   Last of the dwarfish men.

'True was the word I told you:
    Only my son I feared;
For I doubt the sapling courage
    That goes without the beard.
But now in vain is the torture,
    Fire shall never avail:
Here dies in my bosom
    The secret of Heather Ale.'

Christmas at Sea

The sheets were frozen hard, and they cut the naked hand;
The decks were like a slide, where a seaman scarce could
        stand;

The wind was a nor'wester, blowing squally off the sea;
And cliffs and spouting breakers were the only things a-lee.

They heard the surf a-roaring before the break of day;
But 'twas only with the peep of light we saw how ill we lay.
We tumbled every hand on deck instanter, with a shout,
And we gave her the maintops'l, and stood by to go about.
All day we tacked and tacked between the South Head and
  the North;
All day we hauled the frozen sheets, and got no further forth;
All day as cold as charity, in bitter pain and dread,
For very life and nature we tacked from head to head.

We gave the South a wider berth, for there the tide-race
  roared;
But every tack we made we brought the North Head close
  aboard;
So 's we saw the cliffs and houses, and the breakers running
  high,
And the coastguard in his garden, with his glass against his
  eye.

The frost was on the village roofs as white as ocean foam;
The good red fires were burning bright in every 'longshore
  home;
The windows sparkled clear, and the chimneys volleyed out;
And I vow we sniffed the victuals as the vessel went about.

The bells upon the church were rung with a mighty jovial
  cheer;
For it's just that I should tell you how (of all days in the year)
This day of our adversity was blessèd Christmas morn,
And the house above the coastguard's was the house where I
  was born.

O well I saw the pleasant room, the pleasant faces there,
My mother's silver spectacles, my father's silver hair;

And well I saw the firelight, like a flight of homely elves,
Go dancing round the china-plates that stand upon the shelves.

And well I knew the talk they had, the talk that was of me,
30   Of the shadow on the household and the son that went to sea;
And O the wicked fool I seemed, in every kind of way,
To be here and hauling frozen ropes on blessèd Christmas
      Day.

They lit the high sea-light, and the dark began to fall.
'All hands to loose topgallant sails,' I heard the captain call.
'By the Lord, she'll never stand it,' our first mate, Jackson,
      cried.
. . . 'It's the one way or the other, Mr Jackson,' he replied.

She staggered to her bearings, but the sails were new and
      good,
And the ship smelt up to windward just as though she
      understood.
As the winter's day was ending, in the entry of the night,
40   We cleared the weary headland, and passed below the light.

And they heaved a mighty breath, every soul on board but
      me,
As they saw her nose again pointing handsome out to sea;
But all that I could think of, in the darkness and the cold,
Was just that I was leaving home and my folks were growing
      old.

UNCOLLECTED POEMS, 1885–1894

The Song of the Sword of Alan

FROM 'KIDNAPPED'

This is the song of the sword of Alan:
The smith made it,
The fire set it;
Now it shines in the hand of Alan Breck.

Their eyes were many and bright,
Swift were they to behold,
Many the hands they guided:
The sword was alone.

The dun deer troop over the hill,
They are many, the hill is one:
The dun deer vanish,
The hill remains.

Come to me from the hills of heather,
Come from the isles of the sea.
O far-beholding eagles,
Here is your meat.

The Bour-Tree Den

Clinkum-clank in the rain they ride
Down by the braes and the grey sea-side,
Clinkum-clank by stane and cairn:
Weary fa' their horse-shoe-airn!

Loud on the causey, saft on the sand,
Round they rade by the tail of the land,
Round and up by the Bour-Tree Den:
Weary fa' the red-coat men!

Aft hae I gane where they hae rade
10   And straigled in the gowden brooms –
Aft hae I gane, a saikless maid,
    And O! sae bonny as the bour-tree blooms!

Wi' swords and guns they wanton there,
    Wi' red, red coats and braw, braw plumes.
But I gaed wi' my gowden hair,
    And O! sae bonny as the bour-tree blooms!

I ran, a little hempie lass,
In the sand and the bent grass,
Or took and kilted my small coats
20   To play in the beached fisher-boats.

I waded deep and I ran fast,
I was as lean as a lugger's mast,
I was as brown as a fisher's creel,
And I liked my life unco weel.

They blew a trumpet at the cross,
Some forty men, both foot and horse,
A'body cam to hear and see,
And wha, among the rest, but me.

My lips were saut wi' the saut air,
30   My face was brown, my feet were bare,
The wind had ravelled my tautit hair,
And I thought shame to be standing there.

Ae man there in the thick of the throng,
Sat in his saddle, straight and strong.
I looked at him and he at me,
And he was a master-man to see.

    — *And who is this yin? and who is yon*
    That has the bonny lendings on?
    That sits and looks sae braw and crouse?
40   — *Mister Frank o' the Big House!*

I gaed my lane beside the sea;
The wind it blew in bush and tree,
The wind blew in bush and bent:
Muckle I saw, and muckle kent!

Between the beach and the sea-hill,
I sat my lane and grat my fill –
I was sae clarty and hard and dark,
And like the kye in the cow park!

There fell a battle far in the north;
50   The evil news gaed back and forth,
And back and forth by brae and bent
Hider and hunter cam and went:

The hunter clattered horse-shoe-airn
By causey-crest and hill-top cairn;
The hider, in by shag and sheuch,
Crept on his wame and little leuch.

The eastland wind blew shrill and snell,
The stars arose, the gloaming fell,
The firelight shone in window and door
60   When Mr Frank cam here to shore.

He hirpled up by the links and the lane,
And chappit laigh in the back-door-stane.
My faither gaed, and up wi' his han'!
— *Is this Mr Frank, or a beggarman?*

I have mistrysted sair, he said,
But let me into fire and bed,
Let me in for auld lang syne,
And give me a dram of the brandy wine.

They hid him in the Bour-Tree Den,
70   And I thought it strange to gang my lane.
I thought it strange, I thought it sweet,
To gang there on my naked feet,

In the mirk night, when the boats were at sea,
I passed the burn abune the knee.
In the mirk night when the folks were asleep,
I had a tryst in the den to keep.

Late and air', when the folks were asleep,
I had a tryst, a tryst to keep,
I had a lad that lippened to me,
80   And bour-tree blossom is fair to see!

O' the bour-tree leaves I busked his bed,
The mune was siller, the dawn was red:
Was nae man there but him and me, –
And bour-tree blossom is fair to see!

Unco weather hae we been through,
The mune glowered, and the wind blew,
And the rain it rained on him and me,
And bour-tree blossom is fair to see!

Dwelling his lane but house or hauld,
90   Aft he was wet and aft was cauld,
I warmed him wi' my briest and knee, –
And bour-tree blossom is fair to see!

There was nae voice of beast ae man,
But the tree soughed and the burn ran,
And we heard the ae voice of the sea;
Bour-tree blossom is fair to see!

To Katharine de Mattos

With a copy of 'Dr Jekyll and Mr Hyde'

Bells upon the city are ringing in the night;
High above the gardens are the houses full of light;
On the heathy Pentlands is the curlew flying free,
And the broom is blowing bonnie in the north countrie.

It's ill to break the bonds that God decreed to bind,
Still we'll be the children of the heather and the wind.
Far away from home, O, it's still for you and me
That the broom is blowing bonnie in the north countrie!

The Fine Pacific Islands

Heard in a Public-house at Rotherhithe

The jolly English Yellowboy
    Is a 'ansome coin when new,
The Yankee Double-eagle
    Is large enough for two.
O, these may do for seaport towns,
    For cities these may do;
But the dibbs that takes the Hislands
    Are the dollars of Peru:
        O, the fine Pacific Hislands,
10   O, the dollars of Peru!

It's there we buy the cocoanuts
    Mast 'eaded in the blue;
It's there we trap the lasses
    All waiting for the crew;
It's there we buy the trader's rum
    What bores a seaman through . . .
In the fine Pacific Hislands
    With the dollars of Peru:
        In the fine Pacific Hislands
20   With the dollars of Peru!

Now, messmates, when my watch is up,
    And I am quite broached to,
I'll give a tip to 'Evving
    Of the 'ansome thing to do:
Let 'em just refit this sailor-man
    And launch him off anew

To cruise among the Hislands
    With the dollars of Peru:
        In the fine Pacific Hislands
30   With the dollars of Peru!

To Henry James

Adela, Adela, Adela Chart
What have you done to my elderly heart?
Of all the ladies of paper and ink
I count you the paragon, call you the pink.

The word of your brother depicts you in part:
'You raving maniac!' Adela Chart;
But in all the asylums that cumber the ground,
So delightful a maniac was ne'er to be found.

I pore on you, dote on you, clasp you to heart,
10   I laud, love, and laugh at you, Adela Chart,
And thank my dear maker the while I admire
That I can be neither your husband nor sire.

Your husband's, your sire's were a difficult part;
You're a byway to suicide, Adela Chart;
But to read of, depicted by exquisite James,
O, sure you're the flower and quintessence of dames.

Eructavit cor meum

My heart was inditing a goodly matter about Adela Chart

Though oft I've been touched by the volatile dart,
20   To none have I grovelled but Adela Chart,
There are passable ladies, no question, in art –
But where is the marrow of Adela Chart?

I dreamed that to Tyburn I passed in the cart –
I dreamed I was married to Adela Chart:
From the first I awoke with a palpable start,
The second dumbfoundered me, Adela Chart!

The Family

I MOTHER AND DAUGHTER

High as my heart! – the quip be mine
That draws their stature to a line,
My pair of fairies plump and dark,
The dryads of my cattle park.
Here by my window close I sit,
And watch (and my heart laughs at it)
How these my dragon-lilies are
Alike and yet dissimilar.
From European womankind
They are divided and defined
By the free limb and the plain mind,
The nobler gait, the naked foot,
The indiscreeter petticoat;
And show, by each endearing cause,
More like what Eve in Eden was –
Buxom and free, flowing and fine,
In every limb, in every line,
Inimitably feminine.
Like ripe fruit on the espaliers
Their sun-bepainted hue appears,
And the white lace (when lace they wear)
Shows on their golden breast more fair.
So far the same they seem, and yet
One apes the shrew, one the coquette –
A sybil or a truant child.
One runs, with a crop-halo, wild;
And one, more sedulous to please,

Her long dark hair, deep as her knees
And thrid with living silver, sees.
30   What need have I of wealth or fame,
A club, an often-printed name?
It more contents my heart to know
Them going simply to and fro:
To see the dear pair pause and pass
Girded, among the drenching grass,
In the resplendent sun; or hear,
When the huge moon delays to appear,
Their kindred voices sounding near
In the verandah twilight. So
40   Sound ever; so, for ever go
And come upon your small brown feet:
Twin honours to my country seat
And its too happy master lent:
My solace and its ornament!

II THE DAUGHTER, TEUILA, NATIVE NAME FOR ADORNER

Man, child or woman, none from her,
The insatiable embellisher,
Escapes! She leaves, where'er she goes,
A wreath, a ribbon, or a rose:
A bow or else a button changed,
50   Two hairs coquettishly deranged,
Some vital trifle takes the eye
And shows the adorner has been by.
Is fortune more obdurate grown?
And does she leave my dear alone
With none to adorn, none to caress?
Straight on her proper loveliness
She broods and lingers, cuts and carves
With combs and brushes, rings and scarves.
The treasure of her hair she takes;
60   Therewith a new presentment makes.
Babe, Goddess, Naïad of the grot,
And weeps if any like it not!

Her absent, she shall still be found,
A posse of native maids around
Her and her whirring instrument
Collected and on learning bent.
Oft clustered by her tender knees
(Smiling himself) the gazer sees,
Compact as flowers in garden beds,
70   The smiling faces and shaved heads
Of the brown island babes: with whom
She exults to decorate her room,
To draw them, cheer them when they cry,
And still to pet and prettify.
Or see, as in a looking-glass
Her graceful, dimpled person pass,
Nought great therein but eyes and hair,
On her true business here and there;
Her huge, half-naked Staff, intent,
80   See her review and regiment,
An ant with elephants, and how
A smiling mouth, a clouded brow,
Satire and turmoil, quips and tears,
She deals among her grenadiers!
Her pantry and her kitchen squad,
Six-footers all, hang on her nod,
Incline to her their martial chests,
With school-boy laughter hail her jests,
And do her in her kilted dress
90   Obsequious obeisances.
But rather to behold her when
She plies for me the unresting pen!
And while her crimson blood peeps out
Hints a suggestion, halts a doubt –
Laughs at a jest; or with a shy
Glance of a parti-coloured eye
Half brown, half gold, approves, delights
And warms the slave for whom she writes!
So dear, may you be never done
100   Your pretty, busy round to run.

And show, with changing frocks and scents,
Your ever-varying lineaments,
Your saucy step, your languid grace,
Your sullen and your smiling face,
Sound sense, true valour, baby fears,
And bright unreasonable tears:
The Hebe of our ageing tribe:
Matron and child, my friend and scribe!

III

About my fields, in the broad sun
110   And blaze of noon, there goeth one,
Barefoot and robed in blue, to scan
With the hard eye of the husbandman
My harvests and my cattle. Her,
When even puts the birds astir
And day has set in the great woods,
We seek, among her garden roods,
With bells and cries in vain: the while
Lamps, plate, and the decanter smile
On the forgotten board. But she,
120   Deaf, blind, and prone on face and knee,
Forgets time, family and feast
And digs like a demented beast.

IV

Tall as a guardsman, pale as the east at dawn,
Who strides in strange apparel on the lawn?
Rails for his breakfast? routs his vassals out
(Like boys escaped from school) with song and shout?
Kind and unkind, his Maker's final freak,
Part we deride the child, part deride the antique!
See where his gang, like frogs, among the dew
130   Crouch at their duty, an unquiet crew;
Adjust their staring kilts; and their swift eyes
Turn still to him who sits to supervise.

He in the midst, perched on a fallen tree
Eyes them at labour; and, guitar on knee,
Now ministers alarm, now scatters joy,
Now twangs a halting chord – now tweaks a boy.
Thorough in all, my resolute vizier,
Plays both the despot and the volunteer,
Exacts with fines obedience to my laws,
140   – And for his music, too, exacts applause.

V

What glory for a boy of ten,
Who now must three gigantic men,
And two enormous, dapple grey
New Zealand pack-horses, array
And lead, and wisely resolute
Our day-long business execute
In the far shore-side town. His soul
Glows in his bosom like a coal;
His innocent eyes glitter again,
150   And his hand trembles on the rein.
Once he reviews his whole command
And chivalrously planting hand
On hip – a borrowed attitude –
Rides off downhill into the wood.

VI

The old lady (so they say) but I
Admire your young vitality.
Still brisk of foot, still busy and keen
In and about and up and down.
I hear you pass with bustling feet
160   The long verandahs round, and beat
Your bell, and 'Lotu! Lotu!' cry;
Thus calling our queer company
In morning or in evening dim,
To prayers and the oft mangled hymn.

All day you watch across the sky
The silent, shining cloudlands ply,
That, huge as countries, swift as birds,
Beshade the isles by halves and thirds;
Till each with battlemented crest
170 Stands anchored in the ensanguined west,
An Alp enchanted. All the day
You hear the exuberant wind at play,
In vast, unbroken voice uplift
In roaring tree, round whistling clift.

VII

I meanwhile in the populous house apart
Sit, snugly chambered, and my silent art
Uninterrupted, unremitting ply
Before the dawn, by morning lamplight, by
The glow of smelting noon, and when the sun
180 Dips past my westering hill and day is done;
So, bending still over my trade of words,
I hear the morning and the evening birds,
The morning and the evening stars behold;
So there apart I sit as once of old
Napier in wizard Merchiston; and my
Brown innocent aides in home and husbandry,
Wonder askance, *What ails the boss?* they ask,
Him, richest of the rich, an endless task
Before the earliest birds or servants stir
190 *Calls and detains him daylong prisoner?*
He, whose innumerable dollars hewed
This cleft in the boar- and devil-haunted wood,
And bade therein, far seen to seas and skies,
His many-windowed, painted palace rise
Red-roofed, blue-walled, a rainbow on the hill,
A wonder in the forest glade: he still
Unthinkable Aladdin, dawn and dark,
Scribbles and scribbles, like a German clerk.
We see the fact, but tell, O tell us why?
200 My reverend washman and wise butler cry.

And from their lips the unanswered questions drop.
How can he live that does not keep a shop?
And why does he, being acclaimed so rich,
Not dwell with other gentry on the beach?
But harbour, impiously brave,
In the cold, uncanny wood, haunt of the fleeing slave?
The sun and the loud rain here alternate:
Here, in the unfathomable bush, the great
Voice of the wind makes a magnanimous sound.
210   Here, too, no doubt, the shouting doves abound
To be a dainty; here in the twilight stream
That brawls adown the forest, frequent gleam
The jewel-eyes of crawfish. These be good:
Grant them! and can the thing be understood?
That this white chief, whom no distress compels,
Far from all compeers in the mountain dwells?
And finds a manner of living to his wish
Apart from high society and sea fish?
Meanwhile at times the manifold
220   Imperishable perfumes of the past
And coloured pictures rise on me thick and fast
And I remember the white rime, the loud
Lamplitten city, shops and the changing crowd
And I remember home and the old time,
The winding river, the white morning rime,
The autumn robin by the riverside,
That pipes in the grey eve.

'As with heaped bees at hiving time'

As with heaped bees at hiving time
The boughs are clotted, as (ere prime)
Heaven swarms with stars, or the city street
Pullulates with faring feet;
So swarmed my senses once; that now
Repose behind my tranquil brow,

Unsealed, asleep, quiescent, clear;
Now only the vast shapes I hear
Hear – and my hearing slowly fills –
10   Rivers and winds among the twisting hills,
And hearken – and my face is lit –
Life facing; death pursuing it.

'Fixed is the doom; and to the last of years'

Fixed is the doom; and to the last of years
Teacher and taught, friend, lover, parent, child,
Each walks, though near, yet separate; each beholds
His dear ones shine beyond him like the stars.
We also, love, for ever dwell apart;
With cries approach, with cries behold the gulph,
The Unvaulted: as two great eagles that do wheel in air
Above a mountain, and with screams confer,
Far heard athwart the cedars.

                                        Yet the years
10   Shall bring us ever nearer; day by day
Endearing, week by week; till death at last
Dissolve that long divorce. By faith we love,
Not knowledge; and by faith though far removed
Dwell as in perfect nearness, heart to heart.

                                        We but excuse
Those things we merely are; and to our souls
A brave deception cherish.
So from unhappy war a man returns
Unfearing, or the seaman from the deep;
So from cool night and woodlands, to a feast
20   May some one enter, and still breathe of dews,
And in her eyes still wear the dusky night.

To My Wife

Found in the Manuscript of 'Weir of Hermiston'

I saw rain falling and the rainbow drawn
On Lammermuir. Hearkening I heard again
In my precipitous city beaten bells
Winnow the keen sea wind. And here afar,
Intent on my own race and place, I wrote.
    Take thou the writing: thine it is. For who
Burnished the sword, blew on the drowsy coal,
Held still the target higher, chary of praise
And prodigal of censure – who but thou?
So now, in the end, if this the least be good,
If any deed be done, if any fire
Burn in the imperfect page, the praise be thine.

FROM *SONGS OF TRAVEL* (1895)

I *The Vagabond*

To an air of Schubert

Give to me the life I love,
  Let the lave go by me,
Give the jolly heaven above
  And the byway nigh me.
Bed in the bush with stars to see,
  Bread I dip in the river –
There's the life for a man like me,
  There's the life for ever.

Let the blow fall soon or late,
  Let what will be o'er me;
Give the face of earth around
  And the road before me.
Wealth I seek not, hope nor love,
  Nor a friend to know me;
All I seek, the heaven above
  And the road below me.

Or let autumn fall on me
  Where afield I linger,
Silencing the bird on tree,
  Biting the blue finger.
White as meal the frosty field –
  Warm the fireside haven –
Not to autumn will I yield,
  Not to winter even!

Let the blow fall soon or late,
  Let what will be o'er me;
Give the face of earth around,
  And the road before me.
Wealth I ask not, hope nor love,
  Nor a friend to know me;
All I ask the heaven above,
  And the road below me.

III *Youth and Love*

To the heart of youth the world is a highwayside.
Passing for ever, he fares; and on either hand,
Deep in the gardens golden pavilions hide,
Nestle in orchard bloom, and far on the level land
Call him with lighted lamp in the eventide.

Thick as the stars at night when the moon is down,
Pleasures assail him. He to his nobler fate
Fares; and but waves a hand as he passes on,
Cries but a wayside word to her at the garden gate,
10 Sings but a boyish stave and his face is gone.

IV *'In dreams, unhappy, I behold you stand'*

In dreams, unhappy, I behold you stand
          As heretofore:
The unremembered tokens in your hand
          Avail no more.

No more the morning glow, no more the grace,
          Enshrines, endears.
Cold beats the light of time upon your face
          And shows your tears.

He came and went. Perchance you wept a while
          And then forgot.
10 Ah me! but he that left you with a smile
          Forgets you not.

V 'She rested by the Broken Brook'

She rested by the Broken Brook   *[handwritten: ? alliteration]*
   She drank of Weary Well,
She moved beyond my lingering look,
   Ah, whither none can tell!

She came, she went. In other lands,
   Perchance in fairer skies,
Her hands shall cling with other hands,
   Her eyes to other eyes.   *[handwritten: she left you for another]*

She vanished. In the sounding town,
10   Will she remember too?
Will she recall the eyes of brown
   As I recall the blue?

VI 'The infinite shining heavens'

The infinite shining heavens
   Rose and I saw in the night
Uncountable angel stars   *[handwritten: growing ...]*
   Showering sorrow and light.
    [handwritten: all.]
I saw them distant as heaven,
   Dumb and shining and dead,
And the idle stars of the night
   Were dearer to me than bread.   *[handwritten: food as dear]*

Night after night in my sorrow
10   The stars stood over the sea,   *[handwritten: shooting star — ... to ...]*
Till lo! I looked in the dusk
   And a star had come down to me.

VIII 'To you, let snow and roses'

To you, let snow and roses
   And golden locks belong:
These are the world's enslavers,
   Let these delight the throng.
But for her of duskier lustre,
   Whose favour still I wear,
The snow be in her kirtle,
   The rose be in her hair!

The hue of Highland rivers
   Careering, full and cool,
From sable on to golden,
   From rapid on to pool –
The hue of heather-honey,
   The hue of honey-bees,
Shall tinge her golden shoulder,
   Shall gild her tawny knees.

IX 'Let Beauty awake in the morn from beautiful dreams'

Let Beauty awake in the morn from beautiful dreams,
     Beauty awake from rest!
     Let Beauty awake
     For Beauty's sake
In the hour when the birds awake in the brake
     And the stars are bright in the west!

Let Beauty awake in the eve from the slumber of day,
     Awake in the crimson eve!
     In the day's dusk end
     When the shades ascend,
Let her wake to the kiss of a tender friend
     To render again and receive!

3

XI *'I will make you brooches and toys for
        your delight'*

I will make you brooches and toys for your delight
Of bird-song at morning and star-shine at night.
I will make a palace fit for you and me
Of green days in forests and blue days at sea.

I will make my kitchen, and you shall keep your room,
Where white flows the river and bright blows the broom,
And you shall wash your linen and keep your body white
In rainfall at morning and dewfall at night.

And this shall be for music when no one else is near,
10   The fine song for singing, the rare song to hear!
That only I remember, that only you admire,
Of the broad road that stretches and the roadside fire.

XII *We Have Loved of Yore*

To an air of Diabelli

Berried brake and reedy island,
Heaven below, and only heaven above,
Through the sky's inverted azure
    Softly swam the boat that bore our love.
    Bright were your eyes as the day;
        Bright ran the stream,
        Bright hung the sky above.
Days of April, airs of Eden,
    How the glory died through golden hours,
10   And the shining moon arising,
    How the boat drew homeward filled with flowers!
        Bright were your eyes in the night:
        We have lived, my love –
        O, we have loved, my love.

Frost has bound our flowing river,
    Snow has whitened all our island brake,
And beside the winter faggot
    Joan and Darby doze and dream and wake.
        Still, in the river of dreams
20   Swims the boat of love –
        Hark! chimes the falling oar!
And again in winter evens
    When on firelight dreaming fancy feeds,
In those ears of agèd lovers
    Love's own river warbles in the reeds.
        Love still the past, O, my love!
        We have lived of yore,
        O, we have loved of yore.

XIV Mater Triumphans

Son of my woman's body, you go, to the drum and fife,
To taste the colour of love and the other side of life –
From out of the dainty the rude, the strong from out of the
    frail,
Eternally through the ages from the female comes the male.

The ten fingers and toes, and the shell-like nail on each,
The eyes blind as gems and the tongue attempting speech;
Impotent hands in my bosom, and yet they shall wield the
    sword!
Drugged with slumber and milk, you wait the day of the
    Lord.

Infant bridegroom, uncrowned king, unanointed priest,
10 Soldier, lover, explorer, I see you nuzzle the breast.
You that grope in my bosom shall load the ladies with rings,
You, that came forth through the doors, shall burst the doors
    of kings.

XV 'Bright is the ring of words'

Bright is the ring of words
  When the right man rings them,
Fair the fall of songs
  When the singer sings them.
Still they are carolled and said –
  On wings they are carried –
After the singer is dead
  And the maker buried.

Low as the singer lies
10 In the field of heather,
Songs of his fashion bring
  The swains together.
And when the west is red
  With the sunset embers,
The lover lingers and sings
  And the maid remembers.

XVI 'In the highlands, in the country places'

In the highlands, in the country places,,
Where the old plain men have rosy faces,
And the young fair maidens
Quiet eyes;
Where essential silence cheers and blesses,
And for ever in the hill-recesses
Her more lovely music
Broods and dies.

O to mount again where erst I haunted;
10 Where the old red hills are bird-enchanted,
And the low green meadows
Bright with sward;

And when even dies, the million-tinted,
And the night has come, and planets glinted,
Lo, the valley hollow
Lamp-bestarred!

O to dream, O to awake and wander
There, and with delight to take and render,
Through the trance of silence,
20   Quiet breath;
Lo! for there, among the flowers and grasses,
Only the mightier movement sounds and passes;
Only winds and rivers,
Life and death.

XVII *To the Tune of Wandering Willie*

Home no more home to me, whither must I wander?
    Hunger my driver, I go where I must.
Cold blows the winter wind over hill and heather;
    Thick drives the rain, and my roof is in the dust.
Loved of wise men was the shade of my roof-tree.
    The true word of welcome was spoken in the door –
Dear days of old, with the faces in the firelight,
    Kind folks of old, you come again no more.

Home was home then, my dear, full of kindly faces,
10   Home was home then, my dear, happy for the child.
Fire and the windows bright glittered on the moorland;
    Song, tuneful song, built a palace in the wild.
Now, when day dawns on the brow of the moorland,
    Lone stands the house, and the chimney-stone is cold.
Lone let it stand, now the friends are all departed,
    The kind hearts, the true hearts, that loved the place of
    old.

Spring shall come, come again, calling up the moorfowl,
   Spring shall bring the sun and rain, bring the bees and
   flowers;
Red shall the heather bloom over hill and valley,
20   Soft flow the stream through the even-flowing hours;
Fair the day shine as it shone on my childhood –
   Fair shine the day on the house with open door;
Birds come and cry there and twitter in the chimney –
   But I go for ever and come again no more.

7 leaving them

XVIII Winter

In rigorous hours, when down the iron lane
The redbreast looks in vain
For hips and haws,
Lo, shining flowers upon my window-pane
The silver pencil of the winter draws.

When all the snowy hill
And the bare woods are still;
When snipes are silent in the frozen bogs,
And all the garden garth is whelmed in mire,
Lo, by the hearth, the laughter of the logs –
More fair than roses, lo, the flowers of fire! *A fire*

XXI To Sidney Colvin

I knew thee strong and quiet like the hills;
I knew thee apt to pity, brave to endure,
In peace or war a Roman full equipt;
And just I knew thee, like the fabled kings
Who by the loud sea-shore gave judgment forth,
From dawn to eve, bearded and few of words.

What, what, was I to honour thee? A child;
A youth in ardour but a child in strength,
Who after virtue's golden chariot-wheels
10 Runs ever panting, nor attains the goal.
So thought I, and was sorrowful at heart.

Since then my steps have visited that flood
Along whose shore the numerous footfalls cease,
The voices and the tears of life expire.
Thither the prints go down, the hero's way
Trod large upon the sand, the trembling maid's:
Nimrod that wound his trumpet in the wood,
And the poor, dreaming child, hunter of flowers,
20 That here his hunting closes with the great:
So one and all go down, nor aught returns.

For thee, for us, the sacred river waits,
For me, the unworthy, thee, the perfect friend;
There Blame desists, there his unfaltering dogs
He from the chase recalls, and homeward rides;
Yet Praise and Love pass over and go in.
So when, beside that margin, I discard
My more than mortal weakness, and with thee
Through that still land unfearing I advance:
If then at all we keep the touch of joy
30 Thou shalt rejoice to find me altered – I,
O Felix, to behold thee still unchanged.

XXII *'The morning drum-call on my eager ear'*

The morning drum-call on my eager ear
Thrills unforgotten yet; the morning dew
Lies yet undried along my field of noon.
But now I pause at whiles in what I do,
And count the bell, and tremble lest I hear
(My work untrimmed) the sunset gun too soon.

q

XXIII 'I have trod the upward and the
*   downward slope'* ✓

I have trod the upward and the downward slope;   *repeats*
I have endured and done in days before;   ✗   *the up & down*
I have longed for all, and bid farewell to hope;
And I have lived and loved, and closed the door.

he has given up & ended to love?   *closed the door*

XXVI If This Were Faith   ✗

God, if this were enough,
That I see things bare to the buff
And up to the buttocks in mire;
That I ask nor hope nor hire,
Nut in the husk,
Nor dawn beyond the dusk,
Nor life beyond death:
God, if this were faith?

Having felt thy wind in my face
10   Spit sorrow and disgrace,   *7 troubled*
Having seen thine evil doom
In Golgotha and Khartoum,
And the brutes, the work of thine hands,
Fill with injustice lands
And stain with blood the sea:
If still in my veins the glee
Of the black night and the sun
And the lost battle, run:
If, an adept,
20   The iniquitous lists I still accept
With joy, and joy to endure and be withstood,
And still to battle and perish for a dream of good:
God, if that were enough?

If to feel, in the ink of the slough,
And the sink of the mire,
Veins of glory and fire
Run through and transpierce and transpire,
And a secret purpose of glory in every part,
And the answering glory of battle fill my heart;
30   To thrill with the joy of girded men
To go on for ever and fail and go on again,
And be mauled to the earth and arise,
And contend for the shade of a word and a thing not seen
    with the eyes:
With the half of a broken hope for a pillow at night
That somehow the right is the right
And the smooth shall bloom from the rough:
Lord, if that were enough?

XXVIII *To the Muse*

Resign the rhapsody, the dream,
    To men of larger reach;
Be ours the quest of a plain theme,
    The piety of speech.

As monkish scribes from morning break
    Toiled till the close of light,
Nor thought a day too long to make
    One line or letter bright:

many connections to faith & religion

We also with an ardent mind,
10   Time, wealth, and fame forgot,
Our glory in our patience find
    And skim, and skim the pot:

Till last, when round the house we hear
    The evensong of birds,
One corner of blue heaven appear
    In our clear well of words.

Leave, leave it then, muse of my heart!
  Sans finish and sans frame,
Leave unadorned by needless art
20   The picture as it came.

XXXV To My Old Familiars

Do you remember – can we e'er forget? –
How, in the coiled perplexities of youth,
In our wild climate, in our scowling town,
We gloomed and shivered, sorrowed, sobbed and feared?
The belching winter wind, the missile rain,
The rare and welcome silence of the snows,
The laggard morn, the haggard day, the night,
The grimy spell of the nocturnal town,
Do you remember? – Ah, could one forget!

10 As when the fevered sick that all night long
Listed the wind intone, and hear at last
The ever-welcome voice of chanticleer
Sing in the bitter hour before the dawn,
With sudden ardour, these desire the day:
So sang in the gloom of youth the bird of hope:
So we, exulting, hearkened and desired.
For lo! as in the palace porch of life
We huddled with chimeras, from within –
How sweet to hear! – the music swelled and fell,
20 And through the breach of the revolving doors
What dreams of splendour blinded us and fled!

I have since then contended and rejoiced:
Amid the glories of the house of life
Profoundly entered, and the shrine beheld:
Yet when the lamp from my expiring eyes
Shall dwindle and recede, the voice of love
Fall insignificant on my closing ears,
What sound shall come but the old cry of the wind

In our inclement city? what return
30   But the image of the emptiness of youth,
Filled with the sound of footsteps and that voice
Of discontent and rapture and despair?
So, as in darkness, from the magic lamp,
The momentary pictures gleam and fade
And perish, and the night resurges – these
Shall I remember, and then all forget.

pain from youth

XXXVI *'The tropics vanish, and meseems that I'*

The tropics vanish, and meseems that I,
From Halkerside, from topmost Allermuir,
Or steep Caerketton, dreaming gaze again.
Far set in fields and woods, the town I see
Spring gallant from the shallows of her smoke,
Cragged, spired, and turreted, her virgin fort
Beflagged. About, on seaward-drooping hills,
New folds of city glitter. Last, the Forth
Wheels ample waters set with sacred isles,
10   And populous Fife smokes with a score of towns.

a new world

There, on the sunny frontage of a hill,
Hard by the house of kings, repose the dead,
My dead, the ready and the strong of word.
Their works, the salt-encrusted, still survive;
The sea bombards their founded towers; the night
Thrills pierced with their strong lamps. The artificers,
One after one, here in this grated cell,
Where the rain erases and the rust consumes,
Fell upon lasting silence. Continents
20   And continental oceans intervene;
A sea uncharted, on a lampless isle,
Environs and confines their wandering child
In vain. The voice of generations dead

graveyard

passing of time

Summons me, sitting distant, to arise,
My numerous footsteps nimbly to retrace,
And, all mutation over, stretch me down
In that devoted city of the dead.

XXXVII To S. C.

I heard the pulse of the besieging sea
Throb far away all night. I heard the wind
Fly crying and convulse tumultuous palms.
I rose and strolled. The isle was all bright sand,
And flailing fans and shadows of the palm;
The heaven all moon and wind and the blind vault;
The keenest planet slain, for Venus slept.
    The king, my neighbour, with his host of wives,
Slept in the precinct of the palisade;
40 Where single, in the wind, under the moon,
Among the slumbering cabins, blazed a fire,
Sole street-lamp and the only sentinel.
    To other lands and nights my fancy turned –
To London first, and chiefly to your house,
The many-pillared and the well-beloved.
There yearning fancy lighted; there again
In the upper room I lay, and heard far off
The unsleeping city murmur like a shell;
The muffled tramp of the Museum guard
20 Once more went by me; I beheld again
Lamps vainly brighten the dispeopled street;
Again I longed for the returning morn,
The awaking traffic, the bestirring birds,
The consentaneous trill of tiny song
That weaves round monumental cornices
A passing charm of beauty. Most of all,
For your light foot I wearied, and your knock
That was the glad réveillé of my day.
    Lo, now, when to your task in the great house

30   At morning through the portico you pass,
     One moment glance, where by the pillared wall
     Far-voyaging island gods, begrimed with smoke,
     Sit now unworshipped, the rude monument
     Of faiths forgot and races undivined:
     Sit now disconsolate, remembering well
     The priest, the victim, and the songful crowd,
     The blaze of the blue noon, and the huge voice,
     Incessant, of the breakers on the shore.
     As far as these from their ancestral shrine,
40   So far, so foreign, your divided friends
     Wander estranged in body, not in mind.

XXXIX *The Woodman*

     In all the grove, nor stream nor bird
     Nor aught beside my blows was heard,
     And the woods wore their noonday dress –
     The glory of their silentness.
     From the island summit to the seas,
     Trees mounted, and trees drooped, and trees
     Groped upward in the gaps. The green
     Inarboured talus and ravine
     By fathoms. By the multitude,
10   The rugged columns of the wood
     And bunches of the branches stood;
     Thick as a mob, deep as a sea,
     And silent as eternity.
     With lowered axe, with backward head,
     Late from this scene my labourer fled,
     And with a ravelled tale to tell,
     Returned. Some denizen of hell,
     Dead man or disinvested god,
     Had close behind him peered and trod,
20   And triumphed when he turned to flee.
     How different fell the lines with me!

Whose eye explored the dim arcade
Impatient of the uncoming shade –   *scared*
Shy elf, or dryad pale and cold,
Or mystic lingerer from of old:
Vainly. The fair and stately things,
Impassive as departed kings,
All still in the wood's stillness stood,
And dumb. The rooted multitude
30   Nodded and brooded, bloomed and dreamed,
Unmeaning, undivined. It seemed
No other art, no hope, they knew,
Than clutch the earth and seek the blue.
Mid vegetable king and priest   *?*
And stripling, I (the only beast)
Was at the beast's work, killing; hewed
The stubborn roots across, bestrewed
The glebe with the dislustred leaves,
And bade the saplings fall in sheaves;
40   Bursting across the tangled math
A ruin that I called a path,
A Golgotha that, later on,
When rains had watered, and suns shone,
And seeds enriched the place, should bear
And be called garden. Here and there,
I spied and plucked by the green hair   *personification*
A foe more resolute to live,
The toothed and killing sensitive.
He, semi-conscious, fled the attack;
50   He shrank and tucked his branches back;   *? hallucinating*
And straining by his anchor-strand,
Captured and scratched the rooting hand.
I saw him crouch, I felt him bite;
And straight my eyes were touched with sight.
I saw the wood for what it was:
The lost and the victorious cause,
The deadly battle pitched in line,
Saw silent weapons cross and shine:
Silent defeat, silent assault,
60   A battle and a burial vault.

Thick round me in the teeming mud
Briar and fern strove to the blood:
The hooked liana in his gin
Noosed his reluctant neighbours in:
There the green murderer throve and spread,
Upon his mothering victims fed,
And wantoned on his climbing coil.
Contending roots fought for the soil
Like frightened demons: with despair
70   Competing branches pushed for air.
Green conquerors from overhead
Bestrode the bodies of their dead:
The Caesars of the sylvan field,
Unused to fail, foredoomed to yield:
For in the groins of branches, lo!
The cancers of the orchid grow.
Silent as in the listed ring
Two chartered wrestlers strain and cling;
Dumb as by yellow Hooghly's side
80   The suffocating captives died;
So hushed the woodland warfare goes
Unceasing; and the silent foes
Grapple and smother, strain and clasp
Without a cry, without a gasp.
Here also sound thy fans, O God,
Here too thy banners move abroad:
Forest and city, sea and shore,
And the whole earth, thy threshing-floor!
The drums of war, the drums of peace,
90   Roll through our cities without cease,
And all the iron halls of life
Ring with the unremitting strife.

The common lot we scarce perceive.
Crowds perish, we nor mark nor grieve:
The bugle calls – we mourn a few!
What corporal's guard at Waterloo?
What scanty hundreds more or less
In the man-devouring Wilderness?

What handful bled on Delhi ridge?
100   — See, rather, London, on thy bridge
The pale battalions trample by,
Resolved to slay, resigned to die.
Count, rather, all the maimed and dead
In the unbrotherly war of bread.
See, rather, under sultrier skies
What vegetable Londons rise,
And teem, and suffer without sound:
Or in your tranquil garden ground,
Contented, in the falling gloom,
110   Saunter and see the roses bloom.
That these might live, what thousands died!
All day the cruel hoe was plied;
The ambulance barrow rolled all day;
Your wife, the tender, kind, and gay,
Donned her long gauntlets, caught the spud,
And bathed in vegetable blood;
And the long massacre now at end,
See! where the lazy coils ascend,
See, where the bonfire sputters red
120   At even, for the innocent dead.

Why prate of peace? when, warriors all,
We clank in harness into hall,
And ever bare upon the board
Lies the necessary sword.
In the green field or quiet street,
Besieged we sleep, beleaguered eat;
Labour by day and wake o' nights,
In war with rival appetites.
The rose on roses feeds; the lark
130   On larks. The sedentary clerk
All morning with a diligent pen
Murders the babes of other men;
And like the beasts of wood and park,
Protects his whelps, defends his den.

Unshamed the narrow aim I hold;
I feed my sheep, patrol my fold;
Breathe war on wolves and rival flocks,
A pious outlaw on the rocks
Of God and morning; and when time
140   Shall bow, or rivals break me, climb
Where no undubbed civilian dares,
In my war harness, the loud stairs
Of honour; and my conqueror
Hail me a warrior fallen in war.

XL *Tropic Rain*

As the single pang of the blow, when the metal is mingled
        well,
Rings and lives and resounds in all the bounds of the bell,
So the thunder above spoke with a single tongue,
So in the heart of the mountain the sound of it rumbled and
        clung.

Sudden the thunder was drowned – quenched with the levin
        light –
And the angle-spirit of rain laughed out loud in the night.
Loud as the maddened river raves in the cloven glen,
Angel of rain! you laughed and leaped on the roofs of men;
And the sleepers sprang in their beds, and joyed and feared
        as you fell.
You struck, and my cabin quailed; the roof of it roared like a
10   bell,
You spoke, and at once the mountain shouted and shook with
        brooks.
You ceased, and the day returned, rosy, with virgin looks.

And methought that beauty and terror are only one, not two;
And the world has room for love, and death, and thunder,
    and dew;
And all the sinews of hell slumber in summer air;
And the face of God is a rock, but the face of the rock is fair.
Beneficent streams of tears flow at the finger of pain;
And out of the cloud that smites, beneficent rivers of rain.

XLIII   The Last Sight

Once more I saw him. In the lofty room,
Where oft with lights and company his tongue
Was trump to honest laughter, sate attired
A something in his likeness. 'Look!' said one,
Unkindly kind, 'look up, it is your boy!'
And the dread changeling gazed on me in vain.

XLIV   'Sing me a song of a lad that is gone'

Sing me a song of a lad that is gone,
    Say, could that lad be I?
Merry of soul he sailed on a day
    Over the sea to Skye.

Mull was astern, Rum on the port,
    Eigg on the starboard bow;
Glory of youth glowed in his soul:
    Where is that glory now?

Sing me a song of a lad that is gone,
    Say, could that lad be I?
Merry of soul he sailed on a day
    Over the sea to Skye.

10

Give me again all that was there,
　　Give me the sun that shone!
Give me the eyes, give me the soul,
　　Give me the lad that's gone!

Sing me a song of a lad that is gone,
　　Say, could that lad be I?
Merry of soul he sailed on a day
20　　Over the sea to Skye.

Billow and breeze, islands and seas,
　　Mountains of rain and sun,
All that was good, all that was fair,
　　All that was me is gone.

XLV To S. R. Crockett

On receiving a Dedication

Blows the wind today, and the sun and the rain are flying,
　　Blows the wind on the moors today and now,
Where about the graves of the martyrs the whaups are crying,
　　My heart remembers how!

Grey recumbent tombs of the dead in desert places,
　　Standing-stones on the vacant wine-red moor,
Hills of sheep, and the howes of the silent vanished races,
　　And winds, austere and pure.

Be it granted me to behold you again in dying,
10　　Hills of home! and to hear again the call;
Hear about the graves of the martyrs the peewees crying,
　　And hear no more at all.

XLVI Evensong

The embers of the day are red
Beyond the murky hill.
The kitchen smokes: the bed
In the darkling house is spread:
The great sky darkens overhead,
And the great woods are shrill.
So far have I been led,
Lord, by Thy will:
So far I have followed, Lord, and wondered still.

10　The breeze from the embalmèd land
Blows sudden toward the shore,
And claps my cottage door.
I hear the signal, Lord – I understand.
The night at Thy command
Comes. I will eat and sleep and will not question more.

APPENDIX

Note on Scots Language, from Underwoods

The human conscience has fled of late the troublesome domain of conduct for what I should have supposed to be the less congenial field of art: there she may now be said to rage, and with special severity in all that touches dialect; so that in every novel the letters of the alphabet are tortured, and the reader wearied, to commemorate shades of mispronunciation. Now spelling is an art of great difficulty in my eyes, and I am inclined to lean upon the printer, even in common practice, rather than to venture abroad upon new quests. And the Scots tongue has an orthography of its own, lacking neither 'authority nor author.' Yet the temptation is great to lend a little guidance to the bewildered Englishman. Some simple phonetic artifice might defend your verses from barbarous mishandling, and yet not injure any vested interest. So it seems at first; but there are rocks ahead. Thus, if I wish the diphthong *ou* to have its proper value, I may write *oor* instead of *our*; many have done so and lived, and the pillars of the universe remained unshaken. But if I did so, and came presently to *doun*, which is the classical Scots spelling of the English *down*, I should begin to feel uneasy; and if I went on a little farther, and came to a classical Scots word, like *stour* or *dour* or *clour*, I should know precisely where I was – that is to say, that I was out of sight of land on those high seas of spelling reform in which so many strong swimmers have toiled vainly. To some the situation is exhilarating; as for me, I give one bubbling cry and sink. The compromise at which I have arrived is indefensible, and I have no thought of trying to defend it. As I have stuck for the most part to the proper spelling, I append a table of some common vowel sounds which no one need consult; and just to prove that I belong to my age and have in me the stuff of a reformer, I have used modification marks throughout. Thus I can tell myself, not without pride, that I have added a fresh stumbling-block for English readers, and to a page of print in my native tongue, have lent a new uncouthness. *Sed non nobis.*

I note again, that among our new dialecticians, the local habitat of every dialect is given to the square mile. I could not emulate this nicety if I desired; for I simply wrote my Scots as well as I was able, not caring if it hailed from Lauderdale or Angus, from the Mearns or Galloway; if I had ever heard a good word, I used it without shame; and when Scots was lacking, or the rhyme jibbed, I was glad (like my betters) to fall back on English. For all that, I own to a friendly feeling for the tongue of Fergusson and of Sir Walter, both Edinburgh men; and I confess that Burns has always sounded in my ear like something partly foreign. And indeed I am from the Lothians myself; it is there I heard the language spoken about my childhood; and it is in the drawling Lothian voice that I repeat it to myself. Let the precisians call my speech that of the Lothians. And if it be not pure, alas! what matters it? The day draws near when this illustrious and malleable tongue shall be quite forgotten: and Burns's Ayrshire, and Dr Macdonald's Aberdeen-awa', and Scott's brave, metropolitan utterance will be all equally the ghosts of speech. Till then I would love to have my hour as a native Maker, and be read by my own countryfolk in our own dying language: an ambition surely rather of the heart than of the head, so restricted as it is in prospect of endurance, so parochial in bounds of space.

TABLE OF COMMON SCOTTISH VOWEL SOUNDS

ae
ai $\Big\}$ = open A as in rare.

a'
au $\Big\}$ = AW as in law.
aw

ea = open E as in mere, but this with exceptions, as heather = heather, wean = wain, lear = lair.

ee
ei $\Big\}$ = open E as in mere.
ie

oa = open O as in more.

ou = double O as in poor.

ow = OW as in bower.

ui or ü before R = (say roughly) open A as in rare.

ui or ü before any other consonant = (say roughly) close I as in grin.

y = open I as in kite.

i = pretty nearly what you please, much as in English. Heaven guide the reader through that labyrinth! But in Scots it dodges usually from the short I, as in grin, to the open E, as in mere. Find and blind, I may remark, are pronounced to rhyme with the preterite of grin.

NOTES

The following abbreviations are used in the Notes:

Printed Sources of Poems

BBS I and *II 1916*: *Poems by Robert Louis Stevenson: Hitherto Unpublished*, ed. George S. Hellman, 2 vols. (The Bibliophile Society of Boston, 1916). Printed for members only.

BBS III 1921: *Poems by Robert Louis Stevenson: Hitherto Unpublished*, ed. George S. Hellman and William P. Trent (The Bibliophile Society of Boston, 1921). Printed for members only.

Edinburgh 1898: *The Works of Robert Louis Stevenson*, Edinburgh Edition, Vol. XXVIII (1898).

JAS: *Robert Louis Stevenson – Collected Poems*, ed. Janet Adam Smith (London, 1950; revised edition, 1971).

Letters 1899: *Letters of Robert Louis Stevenson to His Family and Friends*, ed. Sidney Colvin (London, 1899).

Pentland 1907: *The Works of Robert Louis Stevenson*, Pentland Edition, Vol. XIII, with Bibliographical Notes by Edmund Gosse (London, 1907).

RLS Teuila 1899: *RLS Teuila*, ed. Isobel Strong, privately printed (1899).

Tusitala I and *II 1923*: *The Works of Robert Louis Stevenson*, Tusitala Edition, *Poems*, Vols. I and II (London, [1923]).

Vailima 1922: *The Works of Robert Louis Stevenson*, Vailima Edition. Vol. XXVI, *Miscellanea* (London, 1922).

Other

Letters: *Letters of Robert Louis Stevenson*, eds. Bradford A. Booth and Ernest Mehew, 8 vols. (New Haven, 1994–6).

UNCOLLECTED POEMS, TO 1885

The Light-Keeper

First published in *Edinburgh 1898*, the poem dates from 1869–70 when Stevenson was training to follow in his father's footsteps as a lighthouse engineer.

'The roadside lined with ragweed, the sharp hills'

Written in 1870. First appeared in *Vailima 1922*, along with five other sonnets representing a very young poet's earnest experimentation with the form.

Spring-Song

Probably written in 1871. It appears in manuscript as No. VIII in an exercise book with fifteen poems, some dated 1870–72. Published in *BBS I 1916*.

Duddingston

The manuscript is dated autumn 1871. Published in *BBS I 1916*. The loch at Duddingston, then on the edge of Edinburgh, was a favourite resort for curlers and skaters. The poem, it seems, is the result of a fragile romance with the daughter of a family acquaintance, sometimes referred to as 'Jenny'. (See Frank McLynn, *Robert Louis Stevenson*, p. 53.)

'The whole day thro', in contempt and pity'

First printed in *BBS III 1921*, and confidently assigned by the editors to 1871. This was the year of the Paris Commune. There is evidence in this and other poems that RLS, friend of prostitutes and instinctive sympathizer with the poor and unfortunate, was stirred by the idea of popular revolt. However, he soon firmly rejected the communist solution – see the poem beginning 'The old chimaeras, old receipts . . .', which follows this one in *Tusitala II 1923*.

'I sit up here at midnight'

First published in *BBS III 1921*. The manuscript is dated December 1871. Both the Boston Bibliophile Society editors and Janet Adam Smith point to RLS's debt to Heine in this and other poems.

Dedication

Published in *BBS I 1916*. The 'fascicle' referred to (l. 2) is the notebook with fifteen poems, including 'Spring-Song' above, in which this one appeared, some dated 1870–72. The addressee is not known.

Epistle to Charles Baxter

Printed whole for the first time in *JAS* in 1950, from a manuscript auctioned at Sotheby's the previous year. It can be dated to 1871–2. It is the last in a sequence of poems all in one manuscript book labelled 'Recruiting Songs', which includes 'The whole day thro' . . .' above. Though hedonistic, this epistle is much more straitlaced than RLS's jocular poems addressed to Baxter in Scots – see below. Baxter was RLS's boon companion in public houses and brothels when both were students at Edinburgh University, shared experience with him as a trainee lawyer and, later, became his lawyer, man of affairs, and steady correspondent – a most important friendship. RLS here adapts to literary English the stanza form, originally medieval, known as 'Standard Habbie', after its first conspicuous use in the seventeenth century by Sir Robert Sempill of Beltrees in an elegy for Habbie Simson, the piper of Kilbarchan. In the eighteenth century Ramsay, Fergusson and Burns made it a bedrock of verse in Scots.

To Charles Baxter

First printed in a very small run, for private issue, in 1896, by T. J. Wise, the bibliographer, master crook and forger. But this is genuine – sent in a letter to Baxter from France dated September 1872: see *Letters*, I, 251–2. The Latin is from Martial, *Epigrams*, V, 20: 'bonosque/soles effugere atque abire sentit,/qui nobis pereunt et imputantur'. ('And he feels the good days are flitting and passing away, our days that perish and are scored to our account.')

To Sydney

First published in *BBS I 1916*. 'Sydney' is a pseudonym for RLS's older cousin, R. A. M. Stevenson, otherwise 'Bob', a painter and art critic and an important friend and influence. The manuscript is dated spring 1872.

'O dull, cold northern sky'

Manuscript dated autumn 1872. First published in *BBS I 1916*.

Ne Sit Ancillae Tibi Amor Pudori

Dated [18]72 in manuscript. First printed in *BBS II 1916*. The title translates as: 'Be not ashamed for your love of the handmaiden.' The housemaid cannot be identified.

To Ottilie

Printed in *BBS I 1916*. The editor surmises, plausibly, that 'Ottilie' is a nickname. It could come from Goethe. 'Ottilie' is one of a quartet of protagonists in Goethe's *Elective Affinities* (*Die Wahlverwandtschaften*) of 1809 – a young and beautiful girl whose loves bring her to tragic early death. It may be that, as *BBS I 1916* further speculates, this is only the fragment of an unfinished poem. However, its coolness and absence of stated 'point' make this an especially haunting lyric as it stands – a premonition of Charlotte Mew.

'A little before me, and hark!'

First printed in *JAS* in 1950 from a manuscript auctioned at Sotheby's in the previous year and now in the Beinecke Library of Yale University. Not dated, but clearly belongs where *JAS* places it, in the early 1870s. It evokes the atmosphere of German *lieder* and would almost fit into Schubert's *Winterreise*.

St Martin's Summer

From the 1870–72 'fascicle' – see the note to 'Spring-Song' above: printed in *BBS I 1916*. St Martin's summer is a late spell of fine weather – the Saint's day is 11 November.

'My brain swims empty and light'

First published in *Vailima 1922*. The provocative (but candid, not affected) sexual references in this poem may help to explain why it arrived in print so late. *JAS* notes the obvious influence of Whitman. RLS had composed, or at least begun, an *Ode to Whitman* in 1871. As he wrote in 1887, he felt indebted to *Leaves of Grass* for its blowing 'into space a thousand cobwebs of genteel and ethical illusion.' (Quoted in *JAS*, 461.)

The Cruel Mistress

Again, first printed in *Vailima 1922*. 'Obermann' (l. 37) is the eponymous and profoundly solitary hero of a novel (1804) by Étienne Pivert de Sénancour (1770–1846), a Swiss follower of Rousseau. The book particularly affected Matthew Arnold – see his poem 'Obermann' – who, in turn, influenced the young RLS. The 'grey new town' (l. 28) may be suggested by Wick, in the far north of Scotland, where RLS had spent some time as a prospective lighthouse engineer in 1868.

Storm

Janet Adam Smith thinks this poem may also draw on memories of Wick. First published in *Vailima 1922*, it is another 'Whitmanesque' experiment in free verse.

Stormy Nights

Vailima 1922. Here we seem half-way between Whitman and Ezra Pound.

Song at Dawn

Vailima 1922. Last-printed of the 'Whitmanesque' experiments.

'I am a hunchback, yellow faced —'

First published in *BBS III 1921*.

'Last night we had a thunderstorm in style'

Published, with a facsimile, in *BBS III 1921*, which suggests 1873 as the date of composition. *JAS* more cautiously places it with other experiments with traditional French forms in the years 1875–9.

To Charles Baxter [in Lallan]

First published in *Letters 1899.* Dated October 1875. Stevenson and Baxter, as young advocates, resorted regularly to the Parliament House in Edinburgh High Street, looking for briefs. 'Peter Dick' (l. 40) is not a proper name. *The Concise Scottish National Dictionary* defines 'peter-dick' as a 'rhythmic pattern of two or three short beats followed by one long, *freq.* beaten out by the feet as a dance step or with the knuckles on a board'.

To the Same

This splendid, dangerous poem stands at an oblique angle to the Scottish tradition of jocular elegy that includes the poem by Sempill of Beltrees (1595–1669), noted under 'Epistle of Charles Baxter' above, which pioneered the 'Standard Habbie' metre that RLS uses. To suggest that a man drinking himself to death by the age of fifty is somehow heroic is to call into question genial Burnsian ethics. To make disquiet still more acute, RLS assimilates Adam with Alexander 'Peden' (l. 29) a celebrated Covenanting (ultra-Presbyterian) preacher of the late seventeenth century, still fondly regarded by the 'unco guid' of RLS's own day. '[W]riter lads' (l. 35) are actual or aspirant Writers to the Signet, equivalent to solicitors in England. 'Spanish Dan' (l. 71) is presumably Don Quixote.

'I saw red evening through the rain'

Dated 1875 in *BBS III 1921*, where it first appeared in print. The editors there speculate that stanzas II and IV are separate, unresolved drafts of the same stanza. But the irregular pattern of repetition in this poem could well be a deliberate, and effective, experiment.

'I who all the winter through'

Dated in manuscript 'last of Feby. 1876'. First published in *BBS I 1916*.

John Cavalier

Curiously, this poem, though first published in *Scribner's Magazine* in January 1922, then in the (purportedly) *Complete Poems* published by Scribner in New York in 1923, was not in *Tusitala I* or *II*. Janet Adam Smith thinks that it was almost certainly written in 1878. RLS came upon Jean Cavalier (1681–1740) on his tour of the Cevennes in the autumn of that year and refers to him in his *Travels with a Donkey* (1879) – 'A baker's apprentice with a genius for war, elected brigadier of Camisards at seventeen, to die at fifty-five the English Governor of Jersey.' RLS was aware of affinities between the Protestant Camisard guerrillas and the die-hard Covenanters of late seventeenth century Scotland, whose enemies (ironically) were the 'Cavaliers' commissioned by the Stewart ('Stuart') Kings to root them, and their Presbyterian principles, out. The Camisard rank and file, he wrote in *Travels . . .* , were 'prophets and disciples . . . eager to fight, eager to pray, listening devoutly to the oracles of brain-sick children . . .'. RLS's nostalgia for what he called 'old times of psalm-singing and blood' takes off, but differs, from Scott's sturdy putting of the Covenanters in their historical place in *Old Mortality* (1816).

Alcaics to H. F. Brown

First published in *Letters 1899*. Horatio Forbes Brown (1854–1926) was a close friend of the man of letters and poet John Addington Symonds, who sojourned at Davos. Stevenson met Brown at Davos in 1880 or 1881 – Brown himself divided his time between Davos and Venice, a city about which he wrote extensively. With Brown and Symonds, RLS discussed classical metres for hours, and their sessions inspired a number of experi-

ments. These Horatian Alcaics were produced in April 1881, after Brown
had returned to Venice and sent RLS, as the poem mentions, 'songs' (l. 9)
– translations of Venetian boat-songs (*Letters*, III, 165–6.)

To Mrs MacMorland

The manuscript, dated '2 February 1881, Davos', was first printed from,
inaccurately, in *BBS I 1916*. Mrs MacMorland, the wife of a Church of
Scotland minister, had been resident in Davos for almost ten years when
RLS met her there in 1880.

Brasheanna

All but the first of these sonnets were first privately printed in A. W.
Rosenbach, *Catalogue of the Books and Manuscripts of Robert Louis Stevenson
in the Library of the late Harry Elkins Widener* (Philadelphia, 1913). No. I
appeared in *The Outlook*, 26 February 1898. RLS sent more 'Brash' poems
than these to Charles Baxter. To his old friend, he consigned from Davos,
in November 1881, 'An Ode [on Brash] by Ben Johnson [(*sic*)], Edgar Allan
Poe, and a bungler.' On 15 December of the same year, RLS wrote to
Charles Baxter nostalgically of Edinburgh University days: 'Ah! what would
I not give to steal this evening with you through the big, echoing, college
archway, and away south under the street lamps, and to dear Brash's, now
defunct! . . . O for ten Edinburgh minutes, sixpence between us, and the
ever glorious Lothian Road, or dear mysterious Leith Walk.' (*Letters*, III,
263–4.)

Thomas Brash & Son were wine and spirit merchants at 44 Clerk Street.
Thomas Brash died in 1873 and his son, also Thomas Brash, carried on the
business only till 1879. The relation of these Thomases to the surly barman
of 'Brasheanna' is not quite clear. RLS and Charles Baxter discussed making
a pamphlet of 'Brasheanna' burlesques, and Charles Baxter had two sonnets
set up in type, sending proofs to RLS at Nice in early 1883. RLS thanked
him in Scots: 'Damned, but its bony! Hoo mony pages will there be, think
ye? Stevison maun hae sent ye the feck o' twenty sangs – fifteen I'se warrant.
Weel, that'll can make thretty pages . . .' (*Letters*, IV, 51).

'Since years ago for evermore'

First published in *BBS I 1916*. Found in a manuscript book with poems
dated 1881–4.

RHYMES TO W. E. HENLEY

Gathered under this name in *JAS*. The poet W. E. Henley (1849–1903) was in the Edinburgh Infirmary, a bedridden invalid, when RLS was introduced to him in 1875. RLS sent him verse light and serious over several years of close friendship.

'Dear Henley, with a pig's snout on'

First published in Sidney Colvin's edition of *Letters of Robert Louis Stevenson* (London, 1911). (See *Letters*, III, 231–3.) Stevenson wrote these verses in Braemar in September 1881 while suffering from an especially bad cold – hence the 'pig's snout' respirator from which he inhaled pinewood oil – *oleum pini sylvestri* (l. 18). Sir Wilfred 'Lawson' (l. 35) was a temperance advocate, much jested about by Henley and Stevenson.

'My letters fail, I learn with grief, to please'

First published in *JAS* in 1950, from a manuscript on an undated scrap of paper.

'We dwell in these melodious days'

First printed, inaccurately, in *Stevenson's Workshop with 29 ms facsimiles*, edited by William P. Trent for the members of the Boston Bibliophile Society in 1921. Janet Adam Smith suggests that the 'falsetto flageolet' (l. 12) may refer to RLS's plans to publish as *Penny Whistles* poems that later appeared in *A Child's Garden of Verses*.

Tales of Arabia

First published in *BBS I 1916*. Janet Adam Smith comments: 'Horatian Alcaics, possibly sent with a copy of *New Arabian Nights* (published August 1882) to H. E. Brown or John Addington Symonds.' See the note on 'Alcaics to H. F. Brown' above.

'Flower god, god of the spring, beautiful, bountiful'

Another experiment in classical metre, first published in *BBS I 1916*, which attributes it to April 1883. *JAS* dates it 1881, 1882 or 1883. The metre is the Horatian fifth Asclepiad.

TRANSLATIONS FROM MARTIAL

Martial (*c.* AD 40–103/4) wrote well over 1,500 surviving short poems and epigrams. RLS translated altogether sixteen of these – Janet Adam Smith believes, at Hyères in 1883–4. All were first printed in Boston – *BBS II 1916*, including '*De M. Antonio*' and '*De Ligurra*'; and *BBS III 1921*, including '*Epitaphium Erotii*'. In draft remarks on translating Martial (there is a facsimile of the much-corrected manuscript opposite p. 176 of *BBS II 1916*), RLS admitted that he had forgotten the 'little Latin I ever knew' and had depended on a very bad French 'crib'. He defended Martial – 'the neatest of versifiers, the wittiest of men' – against what he took to be current critical contempt. Unlike more earnest Victorians, RLS would not have been put off by Martial's frequent obscenity, but his own renderings of the celebrated lament for the child Erotion and the quiet encomium on M. Antonius show that he also valued what the *Oxford Companion to Classical Literature*, ed. M. C. Howatson (second edition, 1989) refers to as Martial's 'occasional tenderness' and 'affection for his friends'. '*Epitaphium Erotii*' is from Martial's Book V, 34; '*De M. Antonio*' is X, 23; and '*De Ligurra*' is XII, 61. RLS's translations are represented, along with those of a remarkable array of other poets, in *Martial in English*, edited by J. P. Sullivan and A. J. Boyle for Penguin (Harmondsworth, 1996).

MORAL EMBLEMS (1882)

Lloyd Osbourne, RLS's stepson, had a toy printing press. From 1880, when they were in California, RLS supplied him with copy. Several little publishing events preceded the two twelve-page pamphlets of *Moral Emblems*, from 'Samuel Osbourne & Co, Davos' for sixpence a copy ('Editions De Luxe', No. 1 ninepence, No. 2 tenpence). Woodcuts by RLS and Fanny Stevenson faced the verses printed here. They were included as an Appendix to *Edinburgh 1898*, in an edition of his works planned with RLS, and so are, in a sense, 'canonical'. Janet Adam Smith suggests that RLS was taking off the *Songs Divine and Moral* of Isaac Watts, the eighteenth-century clergyman and hymnologist, whose books had been part of his childhood. These verses, which seem explicit enough without the amusingly crude woodcuts, also prefigure effects found in later 'light verse' by, *inter alia*, Hilaire Belloc, W. H. Auden and Stevie Smith. 'A Peak in Darien' alludes to Keats's celebrated sonnet 'On First Looking into Chapman's Homer'.

FROM *MORAL TALES* [1882]

Two *Moral Tales* originally destined for the Osbourne press were printed for the first time in *Edinburgh 1898*. RLS made three woodcuts for 'Robin and Ben . . .' in 1882 but the text was not taken beyond typescript and he never illustrated 'The Builder's Doom', a second satire on bourgeois cupidity, nor finished two other tales that he planned.

A CHILD'S GARDEN OF VERSES (1885)

First published in 1885 by Longman's Green and Co., London, the *Child's Garden* verses have since appeared in innumerable selections and complete editions in various languages. RLS began writing them at Braemar in 1881, producing another batch in Nice in 1883. He found them a useful recourse during illnesses when prose was beyond his powers, and several were written in the dark, with his left hand, at Hyères in 1884, when he was laid up with a haemorrhage, sciatica and Egyptian ophthalmia. (See Fanny Stevenson's Prefatory Note in *Tusitala I 1923*, xx.) If some of the most-reprinted verses now seem twee in isolation, the volume read as a whole is suffused with the intensity of a sick man's recall of a lonely childhood haunted by illness, its piratical and military fantasies and its eschatological and night-time terrors – though its background is largely Colinton Manse, then outside Edinburgh, a rural spot by the Water of Leith where he spent happy childhood holidays with his grandparents Jane and Dr Lewis Balfour and varied assortments from his fifty or so first cousins.

The *Child's Garden* verses were first assembled, and printed in proof, as *Penny Whistles*. The volume eventually published added six Envoys to the text but left out nine poems set up in the trial version. (These are also omitted here.)

To Alison Cunningham

'Cummy', RLS's nurse from the age of eighteen months, has been described as a 'religious maniac', instilling grim Calvinistic beliefs in damnation and Hell. But RLS depended on her and loved her. He was prepared to justify dedicating the book to her rather than to his mother, whose ill-health consigned him to Cummy's constant care. Fanny Stevenson wrote (Prefatory Note, *Tusitala I 1923*, xvii–xviii):

My husband has told me of the terrors of the night, when he dared not go to sleep lest he should wake amid the flames of eternal torment ... Cummy, kindly soul, never dreaming of the dire effect of her religious training ... The terrifying aspects of religion were generally confined to the night hours. In the daytime Cummy, with her contagious gaiety and unceasing inventions for the amusement of her nursling, made the time fly on wings. Her imagination was almost as vivid as the child's ...

Young Night Thought

The title here is proof, if any were needed, that RLS wrote with older readers in mind. The *Night Thoughts* in verse of Edward Young (1683–1765), published in 1742–4, were still widely read in the period of RLS's childhood, but not by small children.

Whole Duty of Children

Another title for grown-ups. *The Whole Duty of Man*, a devotional work published anonymously in 1658, had long retained currency.

Where Go the Boats

The 'mill' (l. 10) recalled here was on the Water of Leith, near Colinton Manse.

ENVOYS

'Willie and Henrietta' Traquair were the children of RLS's mother's sister, and he played with them a great deal at Colinton. 'Auntie' was Miss Jane Whyte Balfour, housekeeper for her father, Lewis Balfour, at Colinton

Manse, and ready tenderly to 'mother' up to ten of the Stevenson/Balfour cousinage at a time. 'Minnie' was another Balfour cousin. The 'Name-Child' was Louis Sanchez, son of Nelly Van de Grift, RLS's sister-in-law, who had married Adulpho Sanchez, saloon-keeper at Monterey, California.

FROM *UNDERWOODS* (1887)

Putting *A Child's Garden of Verses* together successfully seems to have encouraged RLS to take his poetry more seriously. He had written to W. E. Henley from Hyères in April 1884: 'You may be surprised to hear that I am now a great writer of verses ... I have the mania now like my betters ... A kind of prose Herrick, divested of the gift of verse, and you behold the Bard. But I like it.' (*Letters*, IV, 267.) He began to send more verses to magazines, so that sixteen of the fifty-four poems in *Underwoods* had appeared in print previously.

When Chatto and Windus published the collection in 1887, Book One consisted of thirty-eight poems in English, Book Two of sixteen, generally longer, poems in Scots – 'my native speech that very dark oracular medium: I suppose this is a folly, but what then?', RLS confided to Henry James from Bournemouth (*c.* 23 December 1886: *Letters*, V, 340). Despite the enduring popularity of the poetry of Burns and the fiction of Scott throughout the English-speaking world, RLS did run the risk of putting off readers baffled by his native idiom, and covered himself with the note on Scots printed in this book as an Appendix above. *Tusitala I* and *II 1923* and other editions of the 1920s offer marginal glosses of Scots words and phrases, neither thoroughly nor, always, accurately.

RLS's friend Edmund Gosse, who reviewed the book at length for *Longman's Magazine* (October 1887) was sympathetic, as were other contemporary critics, but considered, as they did, that RLS's fame would rest on his prose rather than his poetry. He praised RLS's ability to engage the reader in his own voice, as it were, 'in a very confidential spirit', with his own 'theories and moods', and did not object to the inclusion of so many poems addressed to friends – a third of the items in the volume have specific personal direction – but did 'shrink before' RLS's prose Dedication to the book, in which he thanked no fewer than eleven doctors for their help in keeping him alive. (Reprinted in Paul Maixner, ed., *Robert Louis Stevenson: The Critical Heritage*, pp. 273–80.)

The title *Underwoods* was borrowed from Ben Jonson (1572–1637). In a note in *Pentland 1907*, 5, Gosse pointed out that Jonson had explained it as signifying 'a miscellany of "lesser poems of later growth", springing up between the more massive timber of his plays. Stevenson, in his turn, modestly suggested by his adoption of the same title that his little poems were not to prejudice any welcome the world of readers might be prepared to give to his more serious and laboured prose'. Yet RLS here committed to print a great deal of his 'confidential' personality, and conveyed his feeling for 'Lallan' Scots strongly.

BOOK ONE

III The Canoe Speaks

Sent with a letter to Will H. Low from Hyères in the early spring of 1884. Low (1853–1932) was an American artist resident in France. RLS hoped he might illustrate the lines. 'If so, good; if not, hand them on to *Manhattan*, *Cantury* or *Lippincott* at your pleasure, as all these desire my work or pretend to.' However, none of these US magazines printed them. At this point, RLS was 'virtually blind and could only write it in his dark room, with his double green goggles and shade, in pencil scrawl in very large writing' (*Letters*, IV, 264–5).

V The House Beautiful

Absence of commentary on this poem by Janet Adam Smith and others suggests that RLS had no particular house or friend in mind. Though the italicized opening, like certain other verse by RLS, rather strongly anticipates effects in the mature W. B. Yeats, RLS stands forth, uncharacteristically, as a somewhat conventional, though unusually eloquent, Christian moralist, using with ease the octosyllabic couplets associated with Milton's *L'Allegro*. His own house at Hyères, where he probably wrote the poem, was not the one that RLS had in mind. A letter to Will H. Low (March 1883?) from Hyères points to the obvious reference to John Bunyan's allegorical *Pilgrim's Progress*, familiar to RLS in childhood, and much in his mind at this time – see the note to 'To a Gardener' below. Bunyan's Christian, on his way to the Celestial City, pauses at the House Beautiful, whence Prudence, Piety and Charity guide him to the Delectable Mountains. To Low, RLS wrote: '. . . I now draw near to the middle ages; nearly three years ago, that fatal thirty struck; and yet the great work is not yet done – not yet even conceived. But so, as one goes on, the wood seems to thicken, the footpath to narrow, and the House Beautiful on the hill's summit to draw further and further away' (*Letters*, IV, 87).

VI To a Gardener

Janet Adam Smith relates this to a letter to Gosse from Hyères, 20 May 1883: 'This spot, our garden and our view, are sub-celestial. I sing daily with my Bunyan, that great bard, "I dwell already the next door to Heaven!" ' (*Letters*, IV, 125–6.)

IX To K. de M.

Mrs Katharine de Mattos was one of RLS's favourite cousins. 'Katharine' (*Underwoods*, XIX) is also addressed to her.

X To N. V. de G. S.

It is odd that RLS should address a poem suggestive of distant, frustrated love to his wife's sister, Nelly Van de Grift Sanchez, with whom Fanny maintained cordial relations. A family joke?

XII To Mrs Will H. Low

This poem follows XI, 'To Will H. Low' – RLS's painter friend – see note to 'The Canoe Speaks' above. Mrs Low was French. The poem was written at 12 Rue Vernier, Paris, where RLS stayed with the Lows in 1886.

XIII To H. F. Brown

See the note to 'Alcaics to H. F. Brown' above. The book about Venice by Brown to which RLS refers is *Life on the Lagoons* (1884), called 'your fire-surviving roll' (l. 13) because the original manuscript was burnt in a fire at Brown's publishers, Kegan Paul, Trench and Co. – see *JAS*. In contrast with 'T. K. de M.', 'To N. V. de G. S.' and 'To Mrs Will H. Low' above, which are not 'occasional', this poem alludes to very particular matters.

XV Et Tu in Arcadia Vixisti

'And you, too, have lived in Arcadia.' The poem is addressed to RLS's cousin R. A. M. ('Bob') Stevenson (1847–1900), a painter and art critic who had encouraged RLS in his aesthetic and bohemian proclivities. Graham Balfour, *The Life of Robert Louis Stevenson*, dates this poem 1881.

XVI To W. E. Henley

See the note on the chronic invalid Henley under Rhymes to W. E. Henley above. Whereas '*Et Tu in Arcadia Vixisti*' comes close to parody in its use of post-Romantic Parnassian language, fellow feeling with a fellow-sufferer gives this poem strong sincerity.

XVIII The Mirror Speaks

Henry James (1843–1916) first met RLS in Bournemouth in 1885, after the two men had corresponded. 'Skerryvore' (l. 23) – see 'Skerryvore: The Parallel' below – was the name given by RLS to the house in Bournemouth presented to his wife by his father. 'Consuelo' (l. 4) is the heroine of a novel by George Sand (1842) grounded in eighteenth-century musical life. See Janet Adam Smith, *Henry James and Robert Louis Stevenson* (London, 1948).

XXI Requiem

The first intimation of this very famous poem is found in a much longer one written by RLS on a train in August 1879 when he was travelling, in very poor health, to marry Fanny Osbourne in California. George L. Mackay, ed., *The Stevenson Library of Edwin J. Beinecke*, Vol. V, *Manuscripts* (New Haven, 1961), has a facsimile of the manuscript of this, and another of a poem dated '1880 Jan SF [San Francisco]', which has three stanzas. Eliminating the middle stanza left RLS with his *Underwoods* poem.

XXVI The Sick Child

First published in the first number of a short-lived magazine, *The State* on 10 April 1886, with two extra stanzas omitted from the *Underwoods* version.

XXX A Portrait

Edmund Gosse, in *Pentland 1907*, 6, ascribed this poem to RLS's distaste for a 'certain writer' with whom Gosse had witnessed him in a 'clash of temperaments'. RLS's original manuscript makes it clear that this was W. H. Mallock (1849–1923), whose best-known fictional book was *The New Republic* (1877). Mallock was a consistent pamphleteering opponent of Socialist ideas – a kind of counter-Fabian. He published a volume of *Poems* in 1880, which may have been the one that, according to Fanny Stevenson, disgusted RLS particularly as 'excessively morbid and unpleasant in sentiment'. She attributed 'A Portrait' to this reading alone, without naming the author (*Tusitala I 1923*, 55–6.)

BOOK TWO – IN SCOTS

I *The Maker to Posterity*

Regarding the 'Standard Habbie' metre used here, see the note to 'Epistle to Charles Baxter' above. Eleven of the sixteen poems in Book Two of *Underwoods* use this measure. The medieval Scots poets were 'makars', and their present-day descendants still on occasion claim this title. 'Tantallon' (l. 18), in East Lothian, is a ruined castle.

II Ille Terrarum

Written in 1875, and referring to Swanston College, on the Pentland Hills above Edinburgh, of which RLS's father took a lease in 1867.

IV *A Mile an' a Bittock*

Probably written in 1884. Maurice Lindsay, in his *History of Scottish Literature* (London, 1977), p. 305, notes that this poem describes 'the old "Scotch convoy" system, where friends see each other home, walking backwards and forwards for the sake of the talk, and so indefinitely delaying the actual parting'.

V *A Lowden Sabbath Morn*

RLS himself noted, in *Underwoods*:

It may be guessed by some that I had a certain parish in my eye, and this makes it proper I should add a word of disclamation. In my time there have been two ministers in that parish. Of the first I have a special reason to speak well, even if there had been any to think ill. The second I have often met in private and long (in the due phrase) 'sat under' in his church, and neither here nor there have I heard an unkind or ugly word upon his lips. The preacher of the text had thus no original in that particular parish, but when I was a boy, he might have been observed in many others; he was then (like the schoolmaster) abroad; and by recent advices it would seem he has not yet entirely disappeared.

The poem as printed was reduced from a longer manuscript – see *BBS II 1916*.

VI   *The Spaewife*

RLS probably had a specific tune in mind. Fanny Stevenson, in her Prefatory Note published in *Tusitala I 1923*, 59, reports that a Scot domiciled in San Francisco had sent her a tune – which she printed – fitting the 'peculiar movement of the poem' exactly.

X   *Their Laureate to an Academy Class Dinner Club*

When RLS went to Edinburgh Academy in 1861, he spent a year and a half under a master, D'Arcy Thompson, whose class moved up the school with him – always 'the Thamson class'. This poem, written for the 1885 reunion dinner, was printed and distributed as a leaflet. Verses by RLS for the 1875 and 1883 dinners have also survived – *JAS* prints the 1875 set.

XI   *Embro Hie Kirk*

The relaxation, in the second half of the nineteenth century, of Presbyterian suspicion of music and art in churches naturally provoked fundamentalist reactions of the kind satirized here. The poem alludes to the controversy over the installation of an organ – 'kist o' whustles' (l. 53) – in St Giles High Kirk (Cathedral) in 1883.

XII   *The Scotsman's Return from Abroad*

According to RLS's widow, this poem 'was written to amuse his father when we were stopping with the family in Strathpeffer, a dreary "hydro-

pathic" [spa] in the Highlands'. (*Tusitala I 1923*, 55.) RLS and his friend
Charles Baxter had invented 'Thomson' and 'Johnstone' as roles for them-
selves in their student days, and later assumed or referred to these characters
in some of their correspondence. (See *Letters*, IV, 51–2 and *Letters*, V, 30–
31). The target of (affectionate) mockery is the middling Edinburgh middle
class. The 'U.P.' (l. 26) – United Presbyterian – Church had united several
once-extremist sects, but was itself quite moderate, as Mr Thomson notes
and deplores, before the minister 'sweeps' into traditional hell-fire preach-
ing. RLS's own family represented the contradiction, among the Scottish
middle class, between high-Victorian prosperity and the puritanical
Calvinist tradition still adhered to by many of its beneficiaries.

XV To Doctor John Brown

RLS was writing this in December 1880, but obviously added the introduc-
tory stanza after the death of Brown in 1882. Born in 1810, Brown was a
medical man who secured a literary reputation with essays gathered as *Horae
Subsecivae* (1858–61), which acquired the status, for a few generations, of
a 'minor classic'. His best-known piece was 'Rab and His Friends', the
deeply sentimental tale of a battered old mastiff devoted to his master
James, an Edinburgh carrier, whose wife Ailie dies after a serious operation
in agonies vividly described. (In this and other writing about dogs, Brown
anticipated the curious Edinburgh cult of 'Greyfriars Bobbie'.) '[G]owff'
(l. 13) – golf – was invented in Scotland, and on Edinburgh's Bruntsfield
Links dates back to the Middle Ages. 'Neil' (l. 30) was Niel Gow, greatest
of Scottish fiddlers (and painted as such by Raeburn), who lived in Perthshire
in the late eighteenth century.

FROM *BALLADS* (1890)

RLS and Fanny spent November and December 1888 on Tahiti as guests
of Ori, the strikingly handsome sub-chief of the village of Tautira. While
there RLS heard the legendary story of Rahéro from his hostess, the
beautiful Princess Moe. He conceived the idea of a book of South Sea
ballads, but added only one to his 'The Song of Rahéro' – the macabre
'Feast of Famine', which digests Marquesan lore much less convincingly
and is not included here. To make up a volume, he threw in three Scottish
narratives. Critical reception of this mixter-maxter was, understandably,
lukewarm.

The Song of Rahéro

The story appealed to RLS's unorthodox understanding of non-Christian, 'savage' morality. He wrote to an old schoolmate, H. B. Baildon, from Vailima in 1891 that his 'Song' was 'a perfect folktale; savage and yet fine, full of a tail foremost morality, ancient as the granite rocks; if the historian, not to say the politician could get that yarn into his head, he would have learned some of his ABC'. For this and other poems in *Ballads* RLS wrote his own notes. This was in the tradition of Scott and Byron, who had presented their verse narratives in clear relation to 'fact' and history. Only a very learned anthropologist could comment authoritatively on RLS's notes to 'The Song of Rahéro': he did take trouble to check the tale with islanders. His own notes to the ballad run:

INTRODUCTION. – This tale, of which I have not consciously changed a single feature, I received from tradition. It is highly popular through all the country of the eight Tevas, the clan to which Rahéro belonged; and particularly in Taiárapu, the windward peninsula of Tahiti, where he lived. I have heard from end to end two versions; and as many as five different persons have helped me with details. There seems no reason why the tale should not be true.

[p. 160, l. 28] 'The aito,' *quasi* champion, or brave. One skilled in the use of some weapon, who wandered the country challenging distinguished rivals and taking part in local quarrels. It was in the natural course of his advancement to be at last employed by a chief, or king; and it would then be a part of his duties to purvey the victim for sacrifice. One of the doomed families was indicated; the aito took his weapon and went forth alone; a little behind him bearers followed with the sacrificial basket. Sometimes the victim showed fight, sometimes prevailed, more often, without doubt, he fell. But whatever body was found, the bearers indifferently took up.

[p. 161, ll. 51–8] 'Pai,' 'Honoura,' and 'Ahupu.' Legendary persons of Tahiti, all natives of Taiárapu. Of the first two, I have collected singular although imperfect legends, which I hope soon to lay before the public in another place. Of Ahupu, except in snatches of song, little memory appears to linger. She dwelt at least about Tepari – 'the sea-cliffs' – the eastern fastness of the isle; walked by paths known only to herself upon the mountains; was courted by dangerous suitors who came swimming from adjacent islands, and defended and rescued (as I gather) by the loyalty of native fish. My anxiety to learn more of 'Ahupu Vehine' became (during my stay in Taiárapua) cause of some diversion to that mirthful people, the inhabitants.

[p. 162, l. 86] 'Covered an oven.' The cooking fire is made in a hole in the ground, and is then buried.

[p. 163, l. 91] 'Flies.' This is perhaps an anachronism. Even speaking of today in Tahiti, the phrase would have to be understood as referring mainly to mosquitoes, and these only in watered valleys with close woods, such as I suppose to form the surroundings of Rahéro's homestead. A quarter of a mile away where the air moves freely, you shall look in vain for one.

[p. 164, l. 121] 'Hook' of mother-of-pearl. Bright-hook fishing, and that with the spear, appear to be the favourite native methods.

[p. 165, l. 139] 'Leaves,' the plates of Tahiti.

[p. 165, l. 150] 'Yottowas,' so spelt for convenience of pronunciation, *quasi* Tacksmen in the Scottish Highlands. The organisation of eight subdistricts and eight yottowas to a division, which was in use (until yesterday) among the Tevas, I have attributed without authority to the next clan: see page [173].

[p. 166, l. 166] 'Ómare,' pronounced as a dactyl. A loaded quarter-staff, one of the two favourite weapons of the Tahitian brave; the javelin, or casting spear, was the other.

[p. 168, l. 208] 'The ribbon of light.' Still to be seen – and heard – spinning from one marae to another on Tahiti; or so I have it upon evidence that would rejoice the Psychical Society.

[p. 169, l. 227] 'Námunu-úra.' The complete name is Námunu-úra te aropa. Why it should be pronounced Námunu, dactyllically, I cannot see, but so I have always heard it. This was the clan immediately beyond the Tevas on the south coast of the island. At the date of the tale the clan organisation must have been very weak. There is no particular mention of Támatéa's mother going to Papara, to the head chief of her own clan, which would appear her natural resource. On the other hand, she seems to have visited various lesser chiefs among the Tevas, and these to have excused themselves solely on the danger of the enterprise. The broad distinction here drawn between Nateva and Námunu-úra is therefore not impossibly anachronistic.

[p. 169, l. 229] 'Hiopa the king.' Hiopa was really the name of the king (chief) of Vaiau; but I could never learn that of the king of Paea – pronounce to rhyme with the Indian *ayah* – and I gave the name where it was most needed. This note must appear otiose indeed to readers who have never heard of either of these two gentlemen; and perhaps there is only one person in the world capable at once of reading my verses and spying the inaccuracy. For him, for Mr Tati Salmon, hereditary high chief of the Tevas, the note is solely written: a small attention from a clansman to his chief.

[p. 169, l. 245] 'Let the pigs be tapu.' It is impossible to explain 'tapu' in a note; we have it as an English word, taboo. Suffice it, that a thing which was 'tapu' must not be touched, nor a place that was 'tapu' visited.

[p. 174, l. 359] 'Fish, the food of desire.' There is a special word in the Tahitian language to signify 'hungering after fish.' I may remark that here is one of my chief difficulties about the whole story. How did king, commons, women and all come to eat together at this feast? But it troubled none of my numerous authorities; so there must certainly be some natural explanation.

[p. 177, l. 434] 'The mustering word of the clan.'

Teva te ua,
Teva te matai!

Teva the wind,
Teva the rain!

[p. 182, ll. 549 and 550] 'The star of the dead.' Venus as a morning star. I have collected much curious evidence as to this belief. The dead retain their taste for a fish diet, enter into copartnery with living fishers, and haunt the reef and the lagoon. The conclusion attributed to the nameless lady of the legend would be reached today, under the like circumstances, by ninety per cent of Polynesians: and here I probably understate by one-tenth.

Ticonderoga

Fanny Stevenson, in her Prefatory Note published in *Tusitala I 1923*, 55, describes how she and RLS were summoned to Edinburgh in 1887 (she says August, but it was in fact May) with the news that his father was dying. After Thomas Stevenson breathed his last on May 7, RLS himself was too ill to go to the funeral.

During the gloomy days that followed, my husband, who occupied the rooms that had been set apart for him in his boyhood, with the many evidences of his father's affection surrounding him on every side – the books on the shelves, the childish toys still sacredly cherished – found that he must turn his thoughts into other channels, or he would be unable to fulfil the duties that now devolved upon him. He resolutely sat himself at his desk and wrote *The Ballad of Ticonderoga*, the theme of which had already been discussed with his father before that fine intellect had become obscured by the clouds that settled round his last days.

Then RLS left Scotland, for the last time. The poem was issued in a limited edition in Edinburgh at Christmas, 1887. It clearly relates to the closing scenes of *The Master of Ballantrae*, published in 1889. His own note runs:

INTRODUCTION. – I first heard this legend of my own country from that friend of men of letters, Mr Alfred Nutt, 'there in roaring London's central stream,' and since the ballad first saw the light of day in *Scribner's Magazine* Mr Nutt and Lord Archibald Campbell have been in public controversy on the facts. Two clans, the Camerons and the Campbells, lay claim to this bracing story; and they do well: the man who preferred his plighted troth to the commands and menaces of the dead is an ancestor worth disputing. But the Campbells must rest content: they have the broad lands and the broad page of history; this appanage must be denied them; for between the name of 'Cameron' and that of 'Campbell,' the muse will never hesitate.

[p. 185, l. 67] Mr Nutt reminds me it was 'by my sword and Ben Cruachan' the Cameron swore.

[p. 188, l. 159] 'A periwig'd lord of London'. The first Pitt.

[p. 189, l. 204] 'Cathay.' There must be some omission in General Stewart's charming *History of the Highland Regiments*, a book that might well be republished and continued; or it scarce appears how our friend could have got to China.

Heather Ale

RLS's own note runs:

> Among the curiosities of human nature, this legend claims a high place. It is needless to remind the reader that the Picts were never exterminated, and form to this day a large proportion of the folk of Scotland: occupying the eastern and the central parts, from the Firth of Forth, or perhaps the Lammermoors, upon the south, to the Ord of Caithness on the north. That the blundering guess of a dull chronicler should have inspired men with imaginary loathing for their own ancestors is already strange: that it should have begotten this wild legend seems incredible. Is it possible the chronicler's error was merely nominal? that what he told, and what the people proved themselves so ready to receive, about the Picts, was true or partly true of some anterior and perhaps Lappish savages, small of stature, black of hue, dwelling underground – possibly also the distillers of some forgotten spirit? See Mr Campbell's *Tales of the West Highlands*.

W. N. Herbert picks up the idea of 'heather ale' from RLS and runs with it in a long poem, 'Lammer Wine', in *Cabaret McGonagall* (Newcastle, 1996), pp. 21–5.

Christmas at Sea

Published in the *Scots Observer*, 22 December 1888.

UNCOLLECTED POEMS, 1885–1894

The Song of the Sword of Alan

From *Kidnapped* (1886). In Chapter X of the novel, the narrator David Balfour sees Alan Breck run his sword through four adversaries, then sit

down and improvise a Gaelic song. 'I have translated it here, not in verse
... but at least in the King's English. He sang it often afterwards and the
thing became popular; so that I have heard it, and had it explained to me,
many's the time.'

The Bour-Tree Den

Printed in *BBS II 1916* where it is not dated. Most of the text there is set
out in quatrains, as in the ballad tradition, which RLS very consciously
evokes: the rest is rearranged in quatrains in the present edition. The poem
looks not quite 'finished'. It may be related to the composition of *Kidnapped*
(published 1886) in which RLS made free with eighteenth-century Scottish
history as he does here. '[T]he red-coat men' (l. 8) must be Hanoverian
troops deployed against actual or potential Jacobite insurgency: 'a battle
far in the north' (l. 49) would be Culloden (1746), where the Jacobites were
finally defeated. But we are in the Lowlands, not the Gaelic-speaking
Highlands where Hanoverian troops hunted their beaten enemies down as
described. Generalized and imprecise folk history is part of the ballad
tradition.

To Katharine de Mattos

Katharine was the favourite cousin saluted by RLS in two poems
in *Underwoods* – see above. *Dr Jekyll and Mr Hyde* was published in
1886.

The Fine Pacific Islands

First published by RLS's friend Andrew Lang in his *causerie* 'At the
Sign of the Ship' in *Longman's Magazine*, January 1889, with a jocular
introduction coyly acknowledging RLS as author and suggesting August
1888 as the date of composition. Analogies with certain verses by Kipling
are obvious, though RLS probably had not seen the *Departmental Ditties*,
which Kipling published in Calcutta in 1886–9: he wrote in excited admir-
ation to Henry James in December 1890 (*Letters*, VII, 65–6) as if he had
just discovered him.

To Henry James

First published in *Letters 1899*, with its curious anticipation of John Betjeman's 'Subaltern's Love Song'. Sent in a letter to James from Vailima in October 1891. Adela Chart was the tactless heroine of James's story 'The Marriages', published in *Atlantic Monthly* in August 1891.

The Family

On 1 January 1894, RLS wrote to Charles Baxter (*Letters*, VIII, 227):

If I were to get printed off a very few poems which are somewhat too intimate for the public, could you get them run up in some luxurious manner so that blame fools might be induced to buy them in just a sufficient quantity to pay expenses and the thing remain still in a manner private? We could supply photographs for illustrations, and the poems are of Vailima and the family. I should much like to get this done as a surprise for Fanny.

Sections I, II, IV, VII and VIII were first printed by RLS's stepdaughter Isobel Strong in *RLS Teuila 1899*; III, V and VI in *BBS II 1916*. The sequence evokes RLS's household at Vailima, where the verses were written early in 1893 – Fanny and Isobel (I, II, III); Fanny's son Lloyd Osbourne (IV); her grandson Austin Strong (V); RLS's mother (VI); and RLS himself (VII).

'As with heaped bees at hiving time'

First published in *BBS III 1921*. 'Possibly 1891 – 1894', according to Janet Adam Smith who printed the poem, as repeated here, after careful consideration of a manuscript that looks like draft rather than fair copy, omitting four lines that appear in *BBS III 1921* and *Tusitala II 1923*.

'Fixed is the doom; and to the last of years'

First published in *BBS II 1916*.

To My Wife

As Dedication this is premature, since RLS left *Weir of Hermiston* incomplete.

FROM *SONGS OF TRAVEL* (1895)

The idea of a uniform Edinburgh Edition of RLS's work was mooted in 1894. RLS saw an opportunity (*Letters*, VIII, 227) to 'extend *Underwoods* with a lot of unpublished stuff'. Only four of the items in the tentative running order that RLS sent to Edmund Gosse had already been printed in 1889–90 – three in the *Scots Observer*, one in *Scribner's*. Eventually the order was settled by Sidney Colvin. In a note to the posthumously published (December 1894) Vol. XIV of the Edinburgh Edition (p. 276), where the new poems appeared as a third book of *Underwoods*, Colvin wrote:

The following verses are here collected for the first time. The author had tried them in several different orders and under several different titles, as 'Songs and Notes of Travel', 'Vailima', 'Posthumous Poems', etc.; finally leaving their naming and arrangement to the present editor, with the suggestion that they should be added, as Book III to future editions of *Underwoods*.

As Janet Adam Smith (*JAS*, 501) drily notes, 'Why Stevenson should have thought of the title *Posthumous Poems* Colvin does not make clear.' In any case, Colvin's own *Songs of Travel* was the title that stuck, and Chatto and Windus published them as a separate volume in September 1896. Eight years later the composer Ralph Vaughan Williams extended the popularity of eight (eventually nine) of the poems with his song-cycle *Songs of Travel*, including I, IX, XI, III, IV, VI, XVII, XV and XXIII, nowadays performed in that order. (Hear, for instance, Bryn Terfel on DG 445 946–2, 1995). Vaughan Williams's choices represent only the first half of the collection, taking in none of the 'tropical' poems that feature in the second – the 'Travel' of Colvin's title goes far beyond the Scotland of folksong and the Europe of *lieder*. What this exposes is the tension, which RLS released directly in such haunting poems as 'Sing me a song of a lad that is gone' and 'To S. R. Crockett', between a profound nostalgia for Scotland and the considerable pleasures of his new, tropical, frontier home. To have called the collection *Vailima* would have demonstrated the same tension in reverse. That RLS himself was acutely sensitive to music – instrumental, *lieder* and 'folk' – is made explicit in this collection. Fanny wrote (*Tusitala*

I 1923, 56): 'It is said that when Mr Kipling is heard humming a tune he is supposed to be composing a poem to fit the music. I think my husband must have used something of the same method, for in his library I found . . . verses written out to airs that had pleased him.' It is helpful to 'listen' to some of RLS's best lyrics – for example, 'In the highlands, in the country places' – as essentially 'musical' in impetus. This aligns them with the work of French *symbolistes* contemporary with RLS, and their disciple T. S. Eliot. (While Thomas Hardy was profoundly 'musical', he never 'abstracts' his native Wessex as RLS sometimes abstracts Scotland and its 'country places' so that music prevails over particularity.) The numbering and order of the poems here follow Janet Adam Smith who restored two left out by Colvin, putting them where RLS had placed them.

III   Youth and Love

This is the second successive poem of that name in the collection.

XII   We have loved of yore

Fanny Stevenson, in her Prefatory Note printed in *Tusitala I 1923*, prints the score of the 'Air after Diabelli – op. 168, No. 1' to which RLS wrote this. Anton Diabelli, the Austrian composer (1781–1858) is best known for having prompted Beethoven's *33 Variations on a Waltz by Diabelli Op. 120*, for piano (1819–23).

XIV   Mater Triumphans

'Triumphant Mother', one of RLS's more 'imperialistic' poems, should not be associated too closely with the arrival of RLS's own widowed mother to join him in the Pacific in 1888.

XVII   To the Tune of Wandering Willie

With almost no exceptions, the major writers in the Scottish literary tradition relate very closely in their inspiration to the remarkable 'folk' (popular) song of their nation. Robert Burns wrote a set of words to the same traditional tune, and Walter Scott's finest Scots prose is found in 'Wandering Willie's Tale', narrated by a blind fiddler in *Redgauntlet* (1824). Stevenson used some of his own 'Wandering Willie' lines in Chapter

IX of *The Master of Ballantrae* (1889), where the Master himself sings them.

XVIII Winter

Written at Saranac Lake, New York State, in 1887.

XXI To Sidney Colvin

Colvin (1845–1927), Slade Professor of Fine Arts at Cambridge University from 1873 to 1885, was an important figure in RLS's life from their first meeting in 1873, encouraging his talented junior and introducing him to London literary circles. RLS wrote this poem to him in Bournemouth and considered putting it in *Underwoods*. It appeared in *Songs of Travel* as *To –*.

XXVI If This Were Faith

Graham Balfour, *The Life of Robert Louis Stevenson*, dates this poem 1893.

XXXV To My Old Familiars

Sent, like so many RLS poems, in a letter to Charles Baxter, in this case dated February 1890.

XXXVI 'The tropics vanish, and meseems that I'

Mentioned in the same letter to Baxter as contains 'To My Old Familiars' above.

XXXVII To S. C.

Sent to Sidney Colvin with a letter dated 2 December 1889. Colvin went to the British Museum as keeper of the department of prints and drawings in 1884. He had a flat in the East Wing of the Museum and RLS often stayed with him there. The 'Far-voyaging island gods' (l. 32) alluded to were two huge Easter Island statues under the portico of the Museum.

XXXIX The Woodman

RLS's most extensive venture in 'philosophical' poetry of the kind success-
fully essayed by Tennyson, Browning and Arnold, who were regarded as
the 'great' Victorian poets. He composed it in 1890 when he was clearing
jungle to create an estate at Vailima. He wrote to Sidney Colvin on 2 or
3 November 1890 (*Letters*, VII, 27):

My long silent contests in the forests have had a strange effect on me. The unconcealed
vitality of these vegetables, their exuberant number and strength, the attempts – I
can use no other word – of lianas to enwrap and capture the intruder, the awful
silence, the knowledge that all my efforts are only like the performance of an actor,
the thing of a moment, and the wood will silently and swiftly heal them up with
fresh effervescence ... the whole silent battle, murder, and slow death of the
contending forest; weigh upon the imagination.

The experience set him off on the short story that became 'The Beach of
Falesa'.

XL Tropic Rain

RLS had feared tempest more than anything else, since childhood, as he
confided to Colvin in a letter of Christmas-time 1890, describing a Samoan
rainstorm. 'In my hell, it would always blow a gale.' (*Letters*, VII, 59.)

XLIII The Last Sight

Not included by Colvin in *Songs of Travel*, though set up in type with the
other poems sent by RLS. First published in *The Works of Robert Louis
Stevenson*, Thistle Edition (New York, 1902). The poem refers to RLS's
last sight of his father in May 1887.

XLIV 'Sing me a song of a lad that is gone'

'Over the Sea to Skye', the song that RLS adapts here, was not traditional
'folksong', though he seems to have supposed that it was. It was composed
by Miss Annie MacLeod, later Lady Wilson, after hearing, in 1879, a sea
shanty sung on a boat from Toran to Loch Coruisk, on Skye. The shanty
forms part of her tune. The well-known 'Jacobite' words were written by

Sir Harold Boulton, Bt., as late as 1884. Mrs Stevenson (*Tusitala I 1923*, 58–9) included the tune in her Prefatory Note and observed:

The writing of *Over the Sea to Skye* grew out of a visit from one of the last of the old school of Scots gentlewomen, Miss Ferrier . . . Her singing was a great delight to my husband, who would beg for song after song, especially the Jacobite airs, which had always to be repeated several times. The words to one of these seemed unworthy, so he made a new set of verses more in harmony with the plaintive tune . . .

XLV   To S. R. Crockett

Crockett (1860–1914) was a novelist of the 'Kailyard School' of sentimental fiction. At the front of his *The Stickit Minister*, published in 1893, he wrote: 'To Robert Louis Stevenson of Scotland and Samoa I dedicate these stories of that Grey Galloway land where About the Graves of the Martyrs The Whaups are crying – his heart remembers how.' RLS responded gratefully to Crockett in mid August 1893 (*Letters*, VIII, 153–4), sending him these 'three indifferent stanzas'. He wrote to Colvin on 4 September 1893 that Crockett's words 'brought the tears to my eyes every time I looked at them . . . Singular that I should fulfil the Scots Destiny throughout, and live a voluntary exile, and have my head filled with the blessed, beastly place all the time'. The stanzas appeared next year as a prefatory poem in the eighth, limited, edition of Crockett's book, and in all subsequent reprintings.

'Whaups' (l. 3) are curlews; 'peewees' (l. 11) are peewits or lapwings; and 'howes' (l. 7) often misprinted as 'homes', are wide valleys *or* smallish hollows. Stevenson may have remembered Maes Howe in Orkney, a prehistoric subterranean site, as well as, for example, the broad 'Howe of the Mearns' in Kincardineshire. The 'Standing-stones' (l. 6) are prehistoric man-made formations found in several parts of Scotland. The 'martyrs' (l. 3) were the die-hard Covenanters of the later seventeenth century who fought and died for their Presbyterian, Calvinist creed against the troopers of the Stewart ('Stuart') Kings, Charles II and James VII. The 'Old Mortality' who gave his name to Walter Scott's novel about them was an eighteenth-century eccentric dedicated to tending their graves.

Generally evocative as it may be, of nostalgia and 'vanished' times, the poem is still more poignant if one reads from it RLS's love-hate relationship with Scottish Calvinism, the faith of his parents.

The poem keenly anticipates feelings central to Lewis Grassic Gibbon's fictional trilogy of the 1930s, gathered as *A Scots Quair – Sunset Song, Cloud Howe* and *Grey Granite*. Edwin Morgan, in D. Gifford, ed., *History of Scottish Literature*, Vol. III, *The Nineteenth Century* (Aberdeen, 1988), notes

that RLS 'achieves excellence' by using only three Scottish words –
'whaups', 'howes' and 'peewees' – placed one in each of three stanzas, to
maximum effect.

XLVI Evensong

Written at Vailima.

GLOSSARY

abune above
affa over
a-glee obliquely, sidelong
aiblins perhaps
aik oak
air early
airn iron
Aqua-vitae whisky
auld-farrant old-fashioned

bairn child
bauld bold, fierce
beeks basks
bewast to the west of
bield shelter
bigg build
birsles bristles
blads buffets
blae bluish, grey-blue (as humans with cold)
blate bashful
blatter beat with violence
blaudin' buffeting
bogle ghost
bour-tree bower-tree (no particular species)
brae hill
brander grill
brangled confused
braw fine, splendid
bree brow
brunt scorched
buckie 'young buck'
burd-alane quite alone (also, 'an only child')

burkes 'murders', from the notorious Edinburgh criminal executed in 1829
busk prepare
buss bush
but without, lacking
but an' ben the inner and outer parts of a two-room cottage
byke beehive

callant a youth
caller fresh
cangle dispute
canty cheerful, lively, comfortable
cauld-rife cold
causey roadway
caw drive
chalmer chamber
chappit tapped, knocked
chield (young) man
chucky, chucky-stane pebble
clamjamfried crowded
clart mud, dirt, to dirty
clavers gossip
clegs horse-flies
cleiks holds fast to, clutches
coft bought
collieshangie noisy dispute, uproar
cosh snug, cosy
couthy an' bien snug and well-off
cowpit upset, overturned
crackin' talking
crouse bold, confident
crowdie (here) mixture of oatmeal and water

crunklin' crackling
cuddy donkey

daidle to idle, dawdle
danders clinkers, cinders
daw dawn
denty dainty
devel strike with violence
dink (an' perjink') dainty (and precise)
dinted vibrated
dirlin' rattling
donnered dazed
douce-stappin stepping respectably
dour-heartit hard-hearted
dowie dismal
dozened stupefied
draigled bedraggled
dree endure
droukin' drenched, dripping
drouthy thirsty, addicted to drinking
drucken drunken
dung (ajee) knocked (aside)
dunt a blow, to strike

een eyes
eident assiduous, eager
ettle to aim, try

fand found
fash, fashious to vex or bother oneself; annoying, vexatious
feck majority, a great quantity
fegs! indeed!
fells animal skins
ferlie a wonder, strange sight, object of gossip
fisslin' making a rustling noise
flegs flies, rushes off
fleyed frightened
forfochten exhausted
forjaskit exhausted

fush'n nourishment, spiritual force
fyke fidget, trouble
fyle to soil, foul

gang (my lane) go (on my own)
gangrel vagrant
gash sagacious
gaucy handsome, imposing
gate street, way, route, journey
gestering gesturing, strutting, posturing
gey and easy very easy, too damn easy
girrs snarls
glaur mud
gled bird of prey
gleed squinting
gleg nimble, keen
gliff glance, glimpse
goavin' roving, flighty
grat lamented (from 'to greet')
gravit-knot knot in a cravat
grue shudder
guidman head of household
gutsy greedy

haar cold mist or fog, especially the sea-fogs common in eastern Scotland
hairst harvest
hantle tryit just a bit vexed, somewhat perplexed
hauld property holding
hempie wild, romping, roguish
hinderlands buttocks
hirplin' limping
hirsle bustle
hizzie woman (disparaging, cf. 'hussy')
hoast cough
hotchin' restless, eager
howdie midwife

howe broad vale or depression, hollow

hurdles hips

ilka each

ingle fireside, chimney corner

jaw spurt

jo sweetheart

jowe peal

keek peep

kent known

kintry country

kist o' whustles church organ (chest of whistles)

kittle to tease, tickle, ticklish

kye cattle

laigh low

Lallan Lowland Scots language

lane (a' by her lane) alone (all by herself)

lave the remainder

laverock skylark

law (relatively) round hill (or low)

lear learning

leuch laugh

lift sky, heavens

limmer disreputable, loose woman

linkin' tripping along

lintie linnet

lippened trusted, counted on

Lowden Lothian (area surrounding Edinburgh)

lowsent loosened

lunted kindled

lyart variegated, multicoloured

mane moan

may spouse

mear mare

mirk dark, gloom

mischancy risky

mishanters mishaps

mistened leather presumably, a leather-covered whisky flask

mistrysted let down

morn's mornin' tomorrow morning

muckle large

mutches close-fitting caps

neukit established in a corner, as in 'ingleneuk'

on-blaff, on-ding the bangings and buffetings of rain and tempest

orra occasional, extra, spare, miscellaneous

owercome sooth frequently repeated truth

pack thegither closely associated with each other

paiks thrashing, punishment

parochine parish

pentit painted (here, stained glass)

pickle a smallish number of persons or things

pin'd seize ('poind')

pingein whining

pitaty-parin' potato peel

pit-mirk pitch darkness

plats garden plots

pliskies pranks

plowtered dabbled

pockmantie travelling-bag (portmanteau)

poothered powdered

pows heads

pree sample, test, appraise

preen pin

ram-stam headstrong

raw ring of people

rax stretch, reach out

reamin' frothing, foaming
reek smoke
ripin' groping
rowpit sold by auction
rowst arouse, jolt
rowth abundance
rummer glass tumbler
rummlin' rumbling

saikless uninvited, unsought
sappy (of men) unctuous; (of food) full of goodness
scaddit scalded
scart scratch, scrape
scaur precipice, sheer rock
scowtherin' blighting
screed (here) tune
scunnered disgusted
sea-gleds sea-eagles
sicker sure, secure, confident
shag refuse heap
shauchlin' shuffling, shambling
sheuch trench, gutter
shilfa chaffinch
shintie (here) a golf club, compared to the stick used in 'shinty' – Gaelic hockey
shoon shoes
shouther shoulder
shuit dirt (soot)
siller money – not only 'silver'
sindry asunder, or sundry
sinsyne since then
skelloch cry out
skelp a slap, to strike
skink gruel
skirlin' shrieking, whistling, the sound of wind instruments
slockened satiated and slack
smoored smeared
sneckdraw crafty, deceitful person
snell biting
snowkit sniffed

sonsie jolly, comely
soo pig
soop, soopit to sweep, swept
soughed rustled
souple supple
spaewife female fortune-teller
spang (vb.) to leap, bound; (n.) jerk, jolt
speel climb
speir ask
spier see above, 'speir'
spunk spark
stacher stumble
stack stick
stammer stumble, stagger
stap stick
staw, stawsome disgust, nauseating
steer stir
steigh steep
steik to close
stench staunch, uncompromising
stirk young bullock, foolish oaf
stot young bullock, stupid, clumsy person
stotterin' tottering
stour, stoury dust, dusty
stoyt totter
straigled straggled
stramash uproar
straucht straight
sweir lazy, reluctant
syndit rinsed

tack lease
tautit tangled, shaggy-headed
tent heeded
tenty watchful
theek thatch
thir twae those two
thocht ahint a little behind
thole endure
thrang crowded
thrapple throat

thrawes throes, twists, spasms
thrawn obstinate
throu'ther all together
tint lost
tirls (of a drum) beats
tosh friendly
turlin' twirling, spinning
twine divide
tyke dog

unbieldy unsheltered
unco strange, remarkably,
   extremely
U.P. United Presbyterian (a
   nonconformist denomination)

wale choice, to choose
walie specially selected

wame belly
wambles wobbles
wanchancy unlucky
warstle wrestle
waukrif sleepless
wean child
wersh insipid
whammled overturned
whang jerk
wheen few
whilk which
wierd fate
wud mad

yammert chattered
yett gate
yoke on attack

INDEX OF TITLES

INDEX OF FIRST LINES

READ MORE IN PENGUIN

In every corner of the world, on every subject under the sun, Penguin represents quality and variety – the very best in publishing today.

For complete information about books available from Penguin – including Puffins, Penguin Classics and Arkana – and how to order them, write to us at the appropriate address below. Please note that for copyright reasons the selection of books varies from country to country.

In the United Kingdom: Please write to *Dept. EP, Penguin Books Ltd, Bath Road, Harmondsworth, West Drayton, Middlesex UB7 ODA*

In the United States: Please write to *Consumer Sales, Penguin Putnam Inc., P.O. Box 12289 Dept. B, Newark, New Jersey 07101-5289.* VISA and MasterCard holders call 1-800-788-6262 to order Penguin titles

In Canada: Please write to *Penguin Books Canada Ltd, 10 Alcorn Avenue, Suite 300, Toronto, Ontario M4V 3B2*

In Australia: Please write to *Penguin Books Australia Ltd, P.O. Box 257, Ringwood, Victoria 3134*

In New Zealand: Please write to *Penguin Books (NZ) Ltd, Private Bag 102902, North Shore Mail Centre, Auckland 10*

In India: Please write to *Penguin Books India Pvt Ltd, 11 Community Centre, Panchsheel Park, New Delhi 110017*

In the Netherlands: Please write to *Penguin Books Netherlands bv, Postbus 3507, NL-1001 AH Amsterdam*

In Germany: Please write to *Penguin Books Deutschland GmbH, Metzlerstrasse 26, 60594 Frankfurt am Main*

In Spain: Please write to *Penguin Books S. A., Bravo Murillo 19, 1° B, 28015 Madrid*

In Italy: Please write to *Penguin Italia s.r.l., Via Benedetto Croce 2, 20094 Corsico, Milano*

In France: Please write to *Penguin France, Le Carré Wilson, 62 rue Benjamin Baillaud, 31500 Toulouse*

In Japan: Please write to *Penguin Books Japan Ltd, Kaneko Building, 2-3-25 Koraku, Bunkyo-Ku, Tokyo 112*

In South Africa: Please write to *Penguin Books South Africa (Pty) Ltd, Private Bag X14, Parkview, 2122 Johannesburg*

READ MORE IN PENGUIN

A CHOICE OF CLASSICS

Matthew Arnold	**Selected Prose**
Jane Austen	**Emma**
	Lady Susan/The Watsons/Sanditon
	Mansfield Park
	Northanger Abbey
	Persuasion
	Pride and Prejudice
	Sense and Sensibility
William Barnes	**Selected Poems**
Mary Braddon	**Lady Audley's Secret**
Anne Brontë	**Agnes Grey**
	The Tenant of Wildfell Hall
Charlotte Brontë	**Jane Eyre**
	Juvenilia: 1829–35
	The Professor
	Shirley
	Villette
Emily Brontë	**Complete Poems**
	Wuthering Heights
Samuel Butler	**Erewhon**
	The Way of All Flesh
Lord Byron	**Don Juan**
	Selected Poems
Lewis Carroll	**Alice's Adventures in Wonderland**
	The Hunting of the Snark
Thomas Carlyle	**Selected Writings**
Arthur Hugh Clough	**Selected Poems**
Wilkie Collins	**Armadale**
	The Law and the Lady
	The Moonstone
	No Name
	The Woman in White
Charles Darwin	**The Origin of Species**
	Voyage of the Beagle
Benjamin Disraeli	**Coningsby**
	Sybil

READ MORE IN PENGUIN

A CHOICE OF CLASSICS

Edward Gibbon	**The Decline and Fall of the Roman Empire** (in three volumes)
	Memoirs of My Life
George Gissing	**New Grub Street**
	The Odd Women
William Godwin	**Caleb Williams**
	Concerning Political Justice
Thomas Hardy	**Desperate Remedies**
	The Distracted Preacher and Other Tales
	Far from the Madding Crowd
	Jude the Obscure
	The Hand of Ethelberta
	A Laodicean
	The Mayor of Casterbridge
	A Pair of Blue Eyes
	The Return of the Native
	Selected Poems
	Tess of the d'Urbervilles
	The Trumpet-Major
	Two on a Tower
	Under the Greenwood Tree
	The Well-Beloved
	The Woodlanders
George Lyell	**Principles of Geology**
Lord Macaulay	**The History of England**
Henry Mayhew	**London Labour and the London Poor**
George Meredith	**The Egoist**
	The Ordeal of Richard Feverel
John Stuart Mill	**The Autobiography**
	On Liberty
	Principles of Political Economy
William Morris	**News from Nowhere and Other Writings**
John Henry Newman	**Apologia Pro Vita Sua**
Margaret Oliphant	**Miss Marjoribanks**
Robert Owen	**A New View of Society and Other Writings**
Walter Pater	**Marius the Epicurean**
John Ruskin	**Unto This Last and Other Writings**

READ MORE IN PENGUIN

A CHOICE OF CLASSICS

Walter Scott	**The Antiquary**
	Heart of Mid-Lothian
	Ivanhoe
	Kenilworth
	The Tale of Old Mortality
	Rob Roy
	Waverley
Robert Louis Stevenson	**Kidnapped**
	Dr Jekyll and Mr Hyde and Other Stories
	In the South Seas
	The Master of Ballantrae
	Selected Poems
	Weir of Hermiston
William Makepeace Thackeray	**The History of Henry Esmond**
	The History of Pendennis
	The Newcomes
	Vanity Fair
Anthony Trollope	**Barchester Towers**
	Can You Forgive Her?
	Doctor Thorne
	The Eustace Diamonds
	Framley Parsonage
	He Knew He Was Right
	The Last Chronicle of Barset
	Phineas Finn
	The Prime Minister
	The Small House at Allington
	The Warden
	The Way We Live Now
Oscar Wilde	**Complete Short Fiction**
Mary Wollstonecraft	**A Vindication of the Rights of Woman**
	Mary and **Maria** (includes Mary Shelley's **Matilda**)
Dorothy and William Wordsworth	**Home at Grasmere**